Lecture Notes in Economics and Mathematical Systems

Managing Editors: M. Beckmann and H. P. Künzi

Mathematical Economics

159

Some Aspects of the Foundations of General Equilibrium Theory: The Posthumous Papers of Peter J. Kalman

Edited by Jerry Green

Springer-Verlag
Berlin Heidelberg New York 1978

Managing Editors
Prof. Dr. M. Beckmann
Brown University
Providence, RI 02912/USA

Prof. Dr. H. P. Künzi
Universität Zürich
8090 Zürich/Schweiz

Editor
Jerry Green
Harvard University
Department of Economics
1737 Cambridge St.
Cambridge, MA 02138/USA

Library of Congress Cataloging in Publication Data

Kalman, Peter Jason.
Some aspects of the foundations of general equilibrium theory.

(Lecture notes in economics and mathematical systems ; 159 : Mathematical economics)
Bibliography: p.
Includes index.
1. Equilibrium (Economics)--Addresses, essays, lectures. I. Green, Jerry R. II. Title.
III. Series: Lectures notes in economics and mathematical systems ; 159.
HB145.K34 1978 330'.01'8 78-14520

AMS Subject Classifications (1970): 90A15, 90C50

ISBN 3-540-08918-7 Springer-Verlag Berlin Heidelberg New York
ISBN 0-387-08918-7 Springer-Verlag New York Heidelberg Berlin

Printing and binding: Beltz Offsetdruck, Hemsbach/Bergstr.
2142/3140-543210

FOREWORD

Kenneth J. Arrow

It is with sadness for a personal and scholarly loss that I write this introduction to the papers of my late friend, Peter J. Kalman. Peter was devoted to extending our knowledge of the economic world. He accomplished much in his short career but had probably never been more productive and varied in his work than at the moment of his unexpected fatal illness. The papers that follow illustrate the intensity and variety of his work. They represent work in progress and in some cases have not yet received the final polishing they deserve for publication. These papers do not exhaust his current output, for some papers had already been accepted for publication in journals and therefore do not fit into a collection of unpublished papers.

To Peter, scholarship was a cooperative endeavor to push back the areas of ignorance, not a competitive world in which one person's success is another one's failure. The papers in the present volume reflect this attitude in that all are collaborative: with his student, Kuan-Pin Lin, his frequent collaborator over the last few years, Graciela Chichilnisky, and with his colleague and also frequent collaborator, Richard Dusansky. The publishers and I are grateful that these coauthors and friends have authorized reproduction of their joint papers in this volume. Though Peter and I did not write any articles together, we exchanged many thoughts during the period that he worked with me on research projects at Harvard University, from which we both profited.

The range of subjects in the following papers is broad enough, but it underrepresents the full variety of Peter's interests. The different approaches to and aspects of the foundations of general equilibrium theory are found here, including his interest in non-conventional equilibrium concepts and in the uses of differential topology for the study of comparative statics, but his interesting papers on operations research and on various applied topics in economics are reflected only in one paper.

The discerning and sympathetic reader will find behind the formulas and the severe and rigorous scholarship something of the intellectual zest and warm personality of Peter Kalman.

TABLE OF CONTENTS

An Extension of Comparative Statics to a General Class of Optimal Choice Models

by

G. Chichilnisky and P. J. Kalman*

Department of Economics
Harvard University

October 1976

Abstract

We study properties of the solutions to a parametrized constrained optimization problem in Hilbert spaces. A special operator is studied which is of importance in economic theory; sufficient conditions are given for its existence, symmetry, and negative semidefiniteness. The techniques used are calculus on Hilbert spaces and functional analysis.

* This research was supported by NSF Grant GS18174. P. J. Kalman is visiting Harvard University from SUNY at Stony Brook. The authors thank K. J. Arrow and I. Sandberg for helpful suggestions.

Introduction

In a wide number of economic problems the equilibrium values of the variables can be regarded as solutions of a parametrized constrained maximization problem. This occurs in static as well as dynamic models; in the latter case the choice variables are often paths in certain function spaces and thus can be regarded as points in infinite dimensional spaces.

It is sometimes possible to determine qualitative properties of the solutions with respect to changes in the parameters of the model. The study of such properties is often called comparative statics; [15], [2], and [10]. Certain comparative static properties of the maxima have proven to be of particular importance for economic theory, since the works of Slutsky, Hicks, and Samuelson [15]: they have been formulated in terms of symmetry and negative semidefiniteness of a matrix, called the Slutsky-Hicks-Samuelson matrix. A discussion of this matrix and its applications is given in Section 1. The study of these properties in economic theory, however, has so far been restricted to static models where the choice variable and the parameters are elements in Euclidean spaces, and where there is only one constraint. Infinite dimensionality of the choice variables arises naturally from the underlying dynamics of the models. For example, in optimal growth models with continuous time and problems of planning with infinite horizons [4] and also from the existence of infinitely many characteristics of the commodities indexed, for instance, by states of nature in models with uncertainty, by location, etc. Many times these models are formalized as optimization problems with more than one constraint.

It is the purpose of this paper to extend the study of the Slutsky-Hicks-Samuelson operator to a general class of parametrized, constrained optimization problems which appear in recent works in economic theory: the choice variables and parameters belong to infinite dimensional spaces, the objective function to be maximized depends also on parameters, and the optimization is restricted to regions given by many possibly infinite parametrized constraints, linear or not.[1] The results provide a foundation for the study of comparative statics in dynamic models such as optimal growth and other dynamic models [4].

The derivation of the Slutsky operator is more complicated in the case of many constraints, and the operator obtained is of a slightly different nature. One reason is that the "compensation" can be performed in different manners since there are many constraints, as becomes clear in the proof of Theorem 1 and the remark following it. Also, the existence of parameters introduces new effects that do not exist in the classical models; in general, the classical properties are not preserved. Further, since the values of the constraints may be in an infinite dimensional space of sequences (denoted C), the "generalized Lagrangian multiplier" may also be infinite dimensional, in effect, an element of the dual space of C, denoted C^*. To avoid the problem of existence of such dual elements which are not representable by sequences (e.g., purely finite additive measures [8]) and thus

[1] Related work in infinite dimensional commodity spaces has been done for special cases of one linear constraint and no parameters in the objective function by L. Court [7] and Berger [3]. In finite dimensional models, related work for parametrized models with one constraint was done by Kalman [9], and Kalman and Intriligator [10]; Chichilnisky and Kalman studied parametrized multi-constraint problems in [6].

complicate the computations, we work on a Hilbert space of sequences C. Infinite dimensional economic models where the variables are elements of Hilbert spaces have been studied in [4] and [5].

The extension from finite to infinite dimensional choice variables and parameters involves further technical difficulties. In the first place, existence of optimal solutions is harder to obtain since closed and bounded sets in infinite dimensional spaces are not, in general, compact in certain topologies such as the topology of the norm. To avoid this problem, one usually uses certain weak topologies in which norm bounded and closed sets are compact. However, in these topologies, the continuity of the objective functions is more difficult to obtain, and thus the usual proofs of existence of solutions by compactness-continuity arguments may restrict the class of admissible objective functions. However, using the concavity of the objective function and convexity of the set on which the optimization is performed, we prove existence of an optimal solution on norm bounded closed sets[2] or weakly compact sets without requiring the objective function to be weakly continuous, which widens the choice of objective functions. Thus, the existence of a solution can be obtained in more economic models of this type; a useful tool here is the Banach-Saks theorem [14].

In Section 1 sufficient conditions are given for existence and uniqueness of a C^1 solution to a general optimization problem and for existence of a generalized Slutsky-Hicks-Samuelson operator which contains as a special case the operator of classical economic

---

[2] In any reflexive Banach space or Hilbert space, norm bounded and closed sets are weakly compact [8].

models. In Section 2, properties of this operator are studied: a class of objective and constrained functions is shown to preserve the classical properties of symmetry and negative semidefiniteness of the operator, which are, in general, lost in parametrized models, as seen in [10].

Section 1

We now discuss the Slutsky-Hicks-Samuelson operator and its applications. For further references, see, for instance, [15] and [10]. Consider the maximization problem:

$$\text{(P)} \qquad \max_{x} \; f(x, a)$$

$$\text{subject to} \quad g(x, a) = c \quad ,$$

where f is a real valued map defined on a linear space and g is vector valued, defined on a linear space. Under certain assumptions the optimal solution vector x denoted $h(a, c)$ is a C^1 function of the variables a and c, and, as the parameter c varies, the constraints describe a parametrized family of manifolds on which f is being maximized. In neoclassical consumer theory, for instance, f represents a utility function, x consumption of all commodities, a prices of all commodities and c income. In this theory, h is called the demand function for commodities of the consumer. In neoclassical producer theory, f represents the cost function, x inputs, a input prices, and g a production function constrained by an output requirement c; in this theory, h is called the demand function for inputs of the firm. In both these models, $c \in R^+$. Comparative static results relate to the Slutsky-Hicks-Samuelson operator, given by the derivative of the optimal solution h with respect to the parameter a restricted to the manifold given by

$$f(x, a) = r \quad ,$$

parametrized by the real number r, denoted

$$\frac{\partial}{\partial a} h(a, c)|_{f=r} \quad .$$

This operator will also be denoted $S(a, c)$. It is a well known result that in the finite dimensional consumer model under certain assumptions:

(*) $$S(a, c) = \frac{\partial}{\partial a} h(a, c) + h(a, c) \frac{\partial}{\partial a} h(a, c) \quad .$$

Equation (*) is also called the fundamental equation of value. In this case $S(a, c)$ is considered unobservable since it represents changes in the demand due to a price change when utility is assumed to remain constant, but the right hand side represents two observable effects called the price effect and the income effect on the demand, respectively. Analogous operators are found throughout the body of economic theory. Important properties of the $S(a, c)$ operator are its symmetry and negative semidefiniteness. In addition to their empirical implications, the symmetry property (S) is related to the Frobenius property of local integrability of vector fields or preferences and the negative semidefiniteness property (N) is related to problems of stability of the equilibrium.

A natural question is whether the results of neoclassical consumer and producer theory can be obtained for the general classes of constrained optimization models described above. The results of this paper point in this general direction. However, the S and N properties of the $S(a, c)$ matrix are not, in general, preserved in parametrized models [9]; thus, one can at most hope to obtain sufficient conditions of the classes of models (objective functions and constraints) in which these properties are still satisfied. This is discussed in Section 2.

We now formally define the problem: for a given vector of parameters (a, c) we study the solutions of

(1) $$\max_x \ f(x, a)$$

$$\text{restricted by } \ g(x, a) = c \quad .$$

We assume that f and g are twice continuously Frechet differentiable (denoted C^2) real valued and vector valued functions, respectively. For a discussion of Frechet derivatives see, for instance, [12] or [13]. The Frechet derivative generalizes the definition of the Jacobian of a map between finite dimensional spaces. In infinite dimensional Banach spaces there are other possible definitions of derivatives, such as the Gateaux derivative which generalizes the concept of directional derivatives. For our purposes, we use the Frechet derivatives since much of the theory of ordinary derivatives extends to these types of derivatives, and since the implicit function theorem has a satisfactory extension in this case. In the following, all derivatives are Frechet.

We assume that the variable $x \in X$, $a \in A$, where X and A are real Hilbert spaces and that $c \in C$, an ℓ_2 space of sequences[3]. We assume that the spaces X and C have natural positive cones denoted X^+ and C^+, and we denote by X_0^+ the set of vectors in X which are strictly positive.[4] Let τ denote the weak topology on X [8], and let A_1 and C_1 be open subsets of A and C. For any (a,c) in $A_1 \times C_1$, denote by $g_{c,a}$ the set

$$\{x \in X^+ : g(x,a) \le c\} \quad .$$

The Lagrangian of (1), denoted L, is a real valued map on $X \times A_1 \times C_1 \times C^*$ (C^* the dual of C) given by

$$L(x,a,c,\lambda) = f(x,a) + \lambda(g(x,a) - c)$$

where $\lambda \in C^*$ (C is isomorphic to C^*). Let $\psi_1 : X_1 \times A_1 \times C_1 \to C$ be defined by $\psi_1(x,a,c) = g(x,a) - c$, and $\psi_2 : X_1 \times A_1 \times C_1 \times C^* \to \mathscr{L}(X,R)$ (the space of linear functionals from X to R) be defined by

$$\psi_2(x,a,c,\lambda) = \frac{\partial}{\partial x} L(x,a,c,\lambda)$$

where $\frac{\partial}{\partial x} L$ represents the partial derivative of the function L with respect to the variable x, as a function defined on $X_1 \times A_1 \times C_1 \times C^*$

---

[3]See, for instance, [5] for economic models defined on (weighted) $\ell_2[0,\infty)$ spaces, with finite measures on $[0,\infty)$.

[4]If X is, for instance, a sequence space, $x \in X$, $x = (x_t)$, $t = 1,2,\ldots$, then x is <u>positive</u> (denoted $x > 0$), when $x_t \ge 0$ for all t, $(x_t) \ne (0)$, and x is <u>strictly positive</u> or $x \gg 0$, when $x_t > 0$ for all t.
When $X = L^2$, $x = (x(t))$ then $x > 0$ if $x \ne 0$ and $x(t) \ge 0$ a.e. $x \gg 0$ if $x(t) > 0$ a.e. Similarly, for $X = L^2(R^n)$.

with values, in view of the assumptions on f and g, on the dual space of X (denoted X^*) of continuous linear functionals on X [8]. Let $\psi: X_1 \times A_1 \times C_1 \times C^* \to C \times X^*$ be defined by

$$\psi(x, a, c, \lambda) = \left(g(x,a) - c, \frac{\partial}{\partial x} L(x, a, c, \lambda)\right)$$

$$= (\psi_1(x, a, c), \psi_2(x, a, c, \lambda)) \quad .$$

Let X_1 be a neighborhood of X^+.

We now briefly discuss certain special problems involved in the proof of existence of solutions and of the Slutsky-Hicks-Samuelson operator in infinite dimensional cases. In the next result we make use of necessary conditions of an optimum in order to derive the operator S(a, c). These necessary conditions basically entail the existence of a separating hyperplane; in order to prove that they are satisfied in problems defined in Banach spaces one uses a Hahn-Banach type theorem which requires existence of interior points in the regions where the optimization takes place (see, for instance, the discussion in [13]). However, L_p spaces with $1 \leq p \leq \infty$ have positive cones with empty interior. In these cases, however, if the function to be maximized (f) is continuous and is defined on a neighborhood X_1 of the positive cone X^+, the first order condition for a maximum can still be obtained (see footnote 10 below). An important tool for the derivation of the S(a, c) operator is the implicit function theorem in Hilbert spaces [12]. This theorem requires invertibility of certain operators. In [6] the authors investigated these invertibility properties for finite dimensional models and showed that they are "generically" satisfied by using Sard's theorem. Here we assume them; one can refer, for instance, to the work of Kantorovich and Akilov [11] for sufficient conditions on the functions f and g that will yield the required invertibility of certain linear operators in infinite dimensional spaces. This is discussed further in the remarks after Theorem 1. One can also consider extensions of the results of [6] by use of the infinite dimensional version of Sards' theorem [16]. These results will be developed elsewhere, since they exceed the scope of this paper.

THEOREM 1. Let $f: X_1 \times A_1 \to R$ and $g: X_1 \times A_1 \to C_1$ be C^2 functions. For every $a \in A_1$, let $f(\cdot, a)$ be strictly concave and increasing on x, and g be increasing in x.[5] Assume

(i) the set $g_{c,a}$ is a nonempty convex τ-compact subset of X^+,[6]

(ii) g is regular as a function of x,[7]

---

[5] f is increasing in x if $f(x_1) > f(x_2)$ when $x_1 - x_2 \in X_0^+$.

[6] $g_{c,a}$ is weakly compact in X if it is closed and bounded [8]. So, basically, condition (i) can be viewed as a condition of boundedness and closedness of the "technology" represented by the feasible set $g_{c,a}$. Let $\tilde{g}_{c,a} = \{x: g(x,a) = c\}$. Then when g is strictly increasing in x, given that f is strictly increasing also, the maximum of f over $g_{c,a}$ will be attained in this case at $\hat{x}$ in $\tilde{g}_{c,a}$. An example in infinite dimensional spaces where the set $g_{c,a}$ is convex is provided by all the feasible consumption paths obtained from an initial capital stock in an economy with a convex technology, in the usual optimal growth model. In these cases, the constraint g takes the form of a differential (or difference) equation with initial conditions, see [4].

[7] i.e., for all (x_0, a_0) in $X_1 \times A_1$, $\frac{\partial}{\partial x} g(x_0, a_0)$ is onto.

(iii) for each (a, c), $(\partial/\partial(x,\lambda))\psi$ is a top linear isomorphism, and

(iv) the operator Z defined in (6') below, exists for all (x, λ) in $X_1 \times C^*$ with $\psi(x, a, c, \lambda) = 0$.[8]

Then there exists a unique global map $h: A_1 \times C_1 \to X^+$ which is of class C^1 satisfying

$$f(h(a,c), a) = \max_{x \in g_{c,a}} f(x, a) ,$$

and for any choice of compensating constraint there exists a Slutsky-Hicks-Samuelson operator $S: A_1 \times C_1 \to \mathscr{L}(A, X)$ (the space of linear functionals from A to X) given by

$$S(a, c) \equiv \frac{\partial}{\partial a} h + \frac{\partial}{\partial c} h \frac{\partial}{\partial a} g(h, a)$$

satisfying

$$S(a, c) = \frac{\partial}{\partial a} h \Big|_{\bar{f}} + \frac{\partial}{\partial c} h \left(\phi\left(\frac{\partial}{\partial a} g\right) - \mu\left(\frac{\partial}{\partial a} f\right)\right)$$

$$= - \left[\left(\frac{\partial^2}{\partial x^2} L\right)^{-1} + \left(\frac{\partial^2}{\partial x^2} L\right)^{-1} \left(\frac{\partial}{\partial x} g\right) Z \left(\frac{\partial}{\partial x} g\right)\left(\frac{\partial^2}{\partial x^2} L\right)^{-1}\right] \cdot \left(\frac{\partial^2}{\partial x \partial a} L\right) \quad [9]$$

where the operators ϕ, μ are defined in (14') below, provided these operators are well defined for all (x, λ) with $\psi(x, a, c, \lambda) = 0$.

---

[8] This assumption is shown to be "generically" satisfied in finite dimensional versions of these problems in [6] under certain conditions. For a further discussion on the existence of the operator Z, see the remark after the theorem.

[9] We shall not distinguish between an operator and its adjoint.

Proof. Since $g_{c,a}$ is a τ-compact subset of X_0^+ by (i), if $\{x^n\}$ is a sequence in $g_{c,a}$ with $f(x^n, a) \to \sup_{g_{c,a}} f(x, a)$, then there exists a subsequence, denoted also $\{x^n\}$, converging weakly, i.e., $\{x^n\} \overset{\tau}{\to} h$ in $g_{c,a}$ [14]. By the Banach-Saks theorem there exists a subsequence $\{x^{n_k}\}$ such that the sequence of arithmetic means $\{y^{n_k}\}$,

$$y^{n_k} = \frac{x^{n_1} + \ldots + x^{n_k}}{k}$$

converges to h in the norm. By convexity, $y^{n_k} \in g_{c,a}$, and by concavity of $f(\cdot, a)$, $\{y^{n_k}\}$ is a maximizing sequence also. Since f is continuous, h is a maximum on $g_{c,a}$. By (i), $h \in X^+$. We denote h by $h(a, c)$ also. Uniqueness follows from the assumption of strict concavity of $f(\cdot, a)$ on x. Note that, as discussed in footnote 5, h is in $\tilde{g}_{c,a}$.

By [13] (Theorem 1, p. 243) and conditions (ii) and (iii), a necessary condition for $h(a, c)$ to be a maximum is that $\psi = 0$ at $(h(a, c), a, c, \lambda)$ for some $\lambda > 0$ in C^*.[10] Now by condition (iv) and by the implicit function theorem for Banach spaces (see [12]) it follows that $h(a, c)$, which is the solution of system ψ above, is of class C^1.

We now derive the $S(a, c)$ operator.[11] For each $(a, c) \in A_1 \times C_1$, the first order necessary conditions for an optimum are:

---

[10] Note that the fact that f is continuous and defined on X_1, which is a neighborhood of X^+, replaces the condition in [13] of existence of an interior point of X^+.

[11] The approach used here generalizes the approach of Kalman and Intriligator in [10] which is done for one constraint and for finite dimensional spaces

$$\psi_1 = 0 \ , \qquad \text{i.e.,} \quad g(x,a) - c = 0$$

(2) and

$$\psi_2 = 0 \ , \qquad \text{i.e.,} \quad \frac{\partial}{\partial x} L(x,a,c,\lambda) = 0$$

where, for each fixed (a, c),

$$\psi_1 : X_1 \to C$$

$$\psi_2 : X_1 \times C^* \to X^*$$

so that

$$\psi \ : X_1 \times C^* \to C \times X^* \quad .$$

Locally, at the maximum, the differential of (2) can be written as:

$$\left(\frac{\partial}{\partial x} g\right) dx + \left(\frac{\partial}{\partial a} g\right) da - dc = 0$$

(3)

$$\left(\frac{\partial^2}{\partial x^2} f\right) dx + \left(\frac{\partial^2}{\partial x \partial a} f\right) da + \left(\left(\frac{\partial^2}{\partial x^2} g\right) dx\right) \lambda + \left(\left(\frac{\partial^2}{\partial x \partial a} g\right) da\right) \lambda + \left(\frac{\partial}{\partial x} g\right) d\lambda = 0$$

where

$$\left(\left(\frac{\partial^2}{\partial x^2} g\right) dx\right) \lambda \quad \text{denotes} \quad \sum_j \lambda_j \left(\left(\frac{\partial^2}{\partial x^2} g^j\right) dx\right)$$

and similarly for

$$\left(\left(\frac{\partial^2}{\partial x \partial a} g\right) da\right) \lambda \quad .$$

system (3) in turn, can be written as

(4)
$$\begin{pmatrix} 0 & \left(\frac{\partial}{\partial x} g\right) \\ \left(\frac{\partial}{\partial x} g\right) & \left(\frac{\partial^2}{\partial x^2} L\right) \end{pmatrix} \begin{pmatrix} d\lambda \\ dx \end{pmatrix} = \begin{pmatrix} -\left(\frac{\partial}{\partial a} g\right) da + dc \\ -\left(\frac{\partial^2}{\partial x \partial a} L\right) da \end{pmatrix}$$

where as defined above

$$\frac{\partial}{\partial x} L : X_1 \times A_1 \times C_1 \times C^* \to X^*$$

(4')

$$\frac{\partial^2}{\partial x \partial a} L : X_1 \times A_1 \times C_1 \times C^* \to \mathscr{L}(A, X^*)$$

and similarly

$$\frac{\partial^2}{\partial x^2} L : X_1 \times A_1 \times C_1 \times C^* \to \mathscr{L}(X, X^*)$$

so that for each a, c at the maximum h(a, c) and at the corresponding λ,

$$\frac{\partial^2}{\partial x^2} (L(h, a, c, \lambda)) \in \mathscr{L}(X, X^*) \quad .$$

To simplify notation we now denote $(\partial^2/\partial x^2) L$ at $(h(a, c), a, c, \lambda)$ by $(\partial^2/\partial x^2) L$ also; by the assumption of existence of Z, $(\partial^2/\partial x^2) L$ is invertible.[12]

Thus, by (iv),

$$(5) \qquad \begin{pmatrix} d\lambda \\ \\ dx \end{pmatrix} = \begin{pmatrix} 0 & \left(\frac{\partial}{\partial x} g\right) \\ \\ \left(\frac{\partial}{\partial x} g\right) & \left(\frac{\partial^2}{\partial x^2} L\right) \end{pmatrix}^{-1} \begin{pmatrix} -\left(\frac{\partial}{\partial a} g\right) da + dc \\ \\ -\left(\frac{\partial^2}{\partial x \partial a} L\right) da \end{pmatrix}$$

By results of inverting a partioned matrix we have

---

[12]Since X and A are Hilbert spaces and g is convex in the variable x, for each (a, c) the operator $(\partial^2/\partial x^2 L)$ will be negative definite at the (x, λ) which satisfy the first order conditions $\psi(x, a, c, \lambda) = 0$ when x is a maximum, and thus $(\partial^2/\partial x^2) L$ will be invertible.

$$(6)\quad \begin{pmatrix} 0 & \left(\frac{\partial}{\partial x} g\right) \\ \left(\frac{\partial}{\partial x} g\right) & \left(\frac{\partial^2}{\partial x^2} L\right) \end{pmatrix}^{-1} = \left(\begin{array}{c|c} Z & -Z\left(\frac{\partial}{\partial x} g\right)\left(\frac{\partial^2}{\partial x^2} L\right)^{-1} \\ \hline -\left(\frac{\partial^2}{\partial x^2} L\right)^{-1}\left(\frac{\partial}{\partial x} g\right) Z & \left[\left(\frac{\partial^2}{\partial x^2} L\right)^{-1} + \left(\frac{\partial^2}{\partial x^2} L\right)^{-1}\left(\frac{\partial}{\partial x} g\right) Z \left(\frac{\partial}{\partial x} g\right)\left(\frac{\partial^2}{\partial x^2} L\right)^{-1}\right] \end{array}\right)$$

where

$$(6')\qquad Z = -\left[\left(\frac{\partial}{\partial x} g\right)\left(\frac{\partial^2}{\partial x^2} L\right)^{-1}\left(\frac{\partial}{\partial x} g\right)\right]^{-1}$$

From (5) and (6) we obtain

$$(7)\quad dx = \left(\frac{\partial^2}{\partial x^2} L\right)^{-1}\left(\frac{\partial}{\partial x} g\right) Z \left(\left(\frac{\partial}{\partial a} g\right) da - dc\right)$$

$$- \left[\left(\frac{\partial^2}{\partial x^2} L\right)^{-1} + \left(\frac{\partial^2}{\partial x^2} L\right)^{-1}\left(\frac{\partial}{\partial x} g\right) Z \left(\frac{\partial}{\partial x} g\right)\left(\frac{\partial^2}{\partial x^2} L\right)^{-1}\right]\left(\frac{\partial^2}{\partial x \partial a} L\right) da$$

From (7) we obtain

$$(8)\quad \frac{\partial}{\partial a} x = \left(\frac{\partial^2}{\partial x^2} L\right)^{-1}\left(\frac{\partial}{\partial x} g\right) Z \left(\frac{\partial}{\partial a} g\right)$$

$$- \left[\left(\frac{\partial^2}{\partial x^2} L\right)^{-1} + \left(\frac{\partial^2}{\partial x^2} L\right)^{-1}\left(\frac{\partial}{\partial x} g\right) Z \left(\frac{\partial}{\partial x} g\right)\left(\frac{\partial^2}{\partial x^2} L\right)^{-1}\right]\left(\frac{\partial^2}{\partial x \partial a} L\right)$$

and

$$(9)\qquad \frac{\partial}{\partial c} x = - \left(\frac{\partial^2}{\partial x^2} L\right)^{-1}\left(\frac{\partial}{\partial x} g\right) Z$$

We now consider the effect of a "compensated" change in the vector a, obtained by a change in the parameter c, which keeps the value of the objective function constant, i.e., when

$$df = \left(\frac{\partial}{\partial x} f\right) dx + \left(\frac{\partial}{\partial a} f\right) da = 0 \ .$$

From (2), this implies that at the maxima,

$$-\lambda \cdot \left(\frac{\partial}{\partial x} g\right) dx + \left(\frac{\partial}{\partial a} f\right) da = 0 \ . \tag{10}$$

Also,

$$dc = \left(\frac{\partial}{\partial x} g\right) dx + \left(\frac{\partial}{\partial a} g\right) da \tag{11}$$

Hence, by (10) and (11), when df = 0

$$-\lambda \left(dc - \frac{\partial}{\partial a} g \ da\right) + \frac{\partial}{\partial a} f \ da = 0 \tag{12}$$

which implies in particular that when df = 0, the dc^i's are not all linearly independent. We now choose one of the constraints--say the i-th one--to perform the "compensation," i.e., to insure that the optimal vector stays on the surface $f = r$, on which $df = 0$. Then, if c^i is the i-th component of the vector c,[13] in component form, (12) can be rewritten as[14]

$$(13)\quad \left(dc^i - \left(\frac{\partial}{\partial a} g^i\right) da\right) = \frac{1}{\lambda_i}\left(\frac{\partial}{\partial a} f\right) da - \frac{1}{\lambda_i} \sum_{\gamma \neq i} \lambda_\gamma \left(dc^\gamma - \left(\frac{\partial}{\partial a} g^\gamma\right) da\right)$$

Thus (12) and (13) imply that

$$(14)\qquad dc - \left(\frac{\partial}{\partial a} g\right) da \quad , \qquad \text{when } df = 0$$

becomes

$$(14')\qquad \mu\left(\frac{\partial}{\partial a} f\right) da + \phi\left(dc - \left(\frac{\partial}{\partial a} g\right) da\right)$$

---

[13] In a basis of the Hilbert space C. Similarly, locally the dc^i are a "basis" for the cotangent bundle of C at c.

[14] If c is a real number and there is one constraint, Equation (13) becomes

$$(13')\qquad dc - \left(\frac{\partial}{\partial a} g\right) da = \frac{1}{\lambda}\left(\frac{\partial}{\partial a} f\right) da \quad .$$

And, in the classical case, where $a = p$ (price), $g(x, a) = p \cdot x$, $c = I$ (income), x is consumption, (13) becomes

$$(13'')\qquad dI - x \cdot dp = 0 \quad .$$

Note that the "compensation" has the effect of making the components of dc to be not all linearly independent on the surface $f = r$. For instance, in Equation (13), dc^i is a function of all dc^j, $j \neq i$. Note that $\phi(dc) = 0$ does not imply $dc = 0$; the analog of this situation in the classical case is the fact that dI, I = income, is not a "free" real variable any more when $f = \bar{f}$, since $dI = x \cdot dp$. In the classical consumer case the fact that Equation (14), when $df = 0$, becomes (14'), is equivalent to the classical condition that $dc - x \cdot dp$ (c denotes income) becomes zero when $df = 0$; this follows from the fact that $((\partial/\partial a)f) = 0$ in the classical consumer case (since f does not depend on a), and also that ϕ in this case is zero (see, for instance, [15]).

where for each (x, a, c, λ), $\mu : R \to C^*$ is defined by [15]

$$\mu = \left(0, \ldots, 0, \overset{\text{i-th place}}{\frac{1}{\lambda_i}}, 0, \ldots\right)$$

and $\phi : C^* \to C^*$ $(C \cong C^*)$ is defined by

$$\phi = (\phi_{\ell,j})$$

$$\phi_{\ell,j} = 1 \quad \text{if } \ell = j, \ \ell \neq i$$

$$0 \quad \text{if } \ell \neq j \text{ and } \ell \neq i$$

$$\phi_{i,j} = -\frac{\lambda_j}{\lambda_i} \quad \text{if } j \neq i$$

$$\phi_{i,i} = 0 \quad .$$

and where $\phi \equiv 0$ if c is in R.[16]

Therefore, from (7), (14) and (14') (denoting, as usual dx, when $df = 0$, by $dx|_{f=r}$),

---

[15] μ: $R \to C^*$ $(\cong \ell_2)_*$ will be well defined if the conditions $\psi = 0$ holds for $\lambda \gg 0$ in C^* at the maximum. $\lambda \gg 0$ means $\lambda(c) > 0$ for all c in C^+. In [1] sufficient conditions are given for the existence of a strictly positive supporting hyperplane (or Lagrangian multiplier) $\lambda \gg 0$, in a different context.

[16] If C is an $\ell_2[0,\infty)$ space with a finite measure on $[0,\infty)$ given by the density function λ^{-t}, $t \in [0,\infty)$ (λ a constant in $(0, 1)$) as in [4] and [5], then for ϕ to be a well defined continuous operator from ℓ_2 to ℓ_2, a necessary and sufficient condition is that

$$\sum_{j=1}^{\infty} \lambda^{-j} \left(\frac{\lambda_i}{\lambda_j}\right)^2 < \infty$$

for all i.

$$dx\big|_{f=r} = \left(\frac{\partial^2}{\partial x^2} L\right)^{-1}\left(\frac{\partial}{\partial x} g\right) Z\left(-\mu\left(\frac{\partial}{\partial a} f\right) da - \phi\cdot dc + \phi\left(\frac{\partial}{\partial a} g\right) da\right)$$

$$- \left[\left(\frac{\partial^2}{\partial x^2} L\right)^{-1} + \left(\frac{\partial^2}{\partial x^2} L\right)^{-1}\left(\frac{\partial}{\partial x} g\right) Z\left(\frac{\partial}{\partial x} g\right)\left(\frac{\partial^2}{\partial x^2} L\right)^{-1}\right]\left(\frac{\partial^2}{\partial x\partial a} L\right) da$$

and thus, when $\phi(dc) = 0$, one obtains

$$(15) \quad \frac{\partial x}{\partial a}\Big|_{f=r} = \left(\frac{\partial^2}{\partial x^2} L\right)^{-1}\left(\frac{\partial}{\partial x} g\right) Z\left(-\mu\left(\frac{\partial}{\partial a} f\right) + \phi\left(\frac{\partial}{\partial a} g\right)\right)$$

$$- \left[\left(\frac{\partial^2}{\partial x^2} L\right)^{-1} + \left(\frac{\partial^2}{\partial x^2} L\right)^{-1}\left(\frac{\partial}{\partial x} g\right) Z\left(\frac{\partial}{\partial x} g\right)\left(\frac{\partial^2}{\partial x^2} L\right)^{-1}\right]\left(\frac{\partial^2}{\partial x\partial a} L\right)$$

So, by (8), (9) and (15) at the maximum we obtain:

$$(16) \quad \frac{\partial}{\partial a} h + \frac{\partial}{\partial c} h\left(\frac{\partial}{\partial a} g\right) = \frac{\partial h}{\partial a}\Big|_{\bar{f}} + \frac{\partial}{\partial c} h\left(\phi\left(\frac{\partial}{\partial a} g\right) - \mu\left(\frac{\partial}{\partial a} f\right)\right)$$

$$= -\left[\left(\frac{\partial^2}{\partial x^2} L\right)^{-1} + \left(\frac{\partial^2}{\partial x^2} L\right)^{-1}\left(\frac{\partial}{\partial x} g\right) Z\left(\frac{\partial}{\partial x} g\right)\left(\frac{\partial^2}{\partial x^2} L\right)^{-1}\right]\left(\frac{\partial^2}{\partial x\partial a} L\right)$$

$\equiv S(a, c)$, which completes the proof.

Remark

Sufficient conditions for invertibility of the operators $\frac{\partial}{\partial(x,\lambda)}\psi$, and

$$\left(\left(\frac{\partial}{\partial x} g\right)\left(\frac{\partial^2}{\partial x^2} L\right)^{-1}\left(\frac{\partial}{\partial x} g\right)\right)$$

required in Theorem 1 can be obtained in certain cases for instance, by direct examination of these operators, which involve first and second order partial derivatives of the functions f and g. For instance when the spaces X, A and C are sequence spaces, these operators will be given by infinite matrices. Conditions for invertibility of infinite matrices have been studied, for instance, by Kantorovich in [11]. If X, A and C are spaces of L_2 functions on the line, one can use Fourier transform techniques as, for instance, those of [11]. However, invertibility of operators is a delicate point which requires technical considerations of its own; in this case, it requires conditions on the above operators (and thus on f and g) and on the spaces where the problem is defined, depending on the particular nature of the model. Other techniques to study generic invertibility of related operators are given in [6] for finite dimensional spaces, by use of the Sard theorem. These latter results could be extended to infinite dimensional spaces, in certain cases, by use of an infinite dimensional version of the Sard theorem [16].

Section 2.

The classical property of symmetry of the Slutsky-Hicks-Samuelson matrix which in this framework becomes the operator $S(a,c)$ in Section 1, is, in general, not preserved [10]. For certain classes of objective functions and constraints, symmetry of $S(a,c)$ can be recovered, as seen in the next results. These classes of functions have been used in finite dimensional models of the firm, the consumer, and micromonetary models.

In what follows we assume that all spaces are Hilbert spaces of sequences.

PROPOSITION 1. Assume the objective function $f(x,a)$ has the form

(i) $f \equiv \gamma[a \cdot x] + f^1(x) + f^2(a)$ and the constraints $g(x,a)$ have the form

(ii) $g^i \equiv \delta^i[a \cdot x] + g^{i1}(x) + g^{i2}(a), \quad i = 1,2,\ldots,$ and that the conditions of Theorem 1 of Section 1 are satisfied where $a \in A^+ \subset X^{*+}$, $c \in C^+$, $\gamma, \delta^i \in R^+$ and f, g^i have the same properties as f and g of Theorem 1. Then there exists a unique global C^1 solution for Problem (1) of Section 1, and $S(a,c)$ is symmetric.

Proof. In view of (8), (9) and (15), we obtain:

$$S(a,c) \equiv -\left[\left(\frac{\partial^2}{\partial x^2} L\right)^{-1} + \left(\frac{\partial^2}{\partial x^2} L\right)^{-1} \left(\frac{\partial}{\partial x} g\right) Z \left(\frac{\partial}{\partial x} g\right)\left(\frac{\partial^2}{\partial x^2} L\right)^{-1}\right]\left(\frac{\partial^2}{\partial x \partial a} L\right)$$

By computing the operator $(\partial^2/\partial x \partial a)L$ for the above objective and constraint functions we obtain:

$$\frac{\partial^2}{\partial x \partial a} L = \begin{pmatrix} \gamma + \lambda\,\delta & & 0 \\ & \ddots & \\ 0 & & \gamma + \lambda\,\delta \\ & & & \ddots \end{pmatrix}$$

Note that

$$\left[\left(\frac{\partial^2}{\partial x^2} L\right)^{-1} + \left(\frac{\partial^2}{\partial x^2} L\right)^{-1} \left(\frac{\partial}{\partial x} g\right) Z \left(\frac{\partial}{\partial x} g\right)\left(\frac{\partial^2}{\partial x^2} L\right)^{-1}\right]$$

is symmetric. This completes the proof.

PROPOSITION 2. Under the conditions of Proposition 1, $S(a, c)$ is negative semi-definite if $\gamma + \sum_{i=1}^{\infty} \lambda_i \delta^i \geq 0$.

Proof. Negative semi-definiteness of $S(a, c)$ is obtained from the conditions for (i) and (ii) of Proposition 1 as follows:

First we prove that

$$D = \left[\left(\frac{\partial^2}{\partial x^2} L\right)^{-1} + \left(\frac{\partial^2 L}{\partial x^2}\right)^{-1} \left(\frac{\partial}{\partial x} g\right) Z \left(\frac{\partial}{\partial x} g\right)\left(\frac{\partial^2}{\partial x^2} L\right)^{-1}\right]$$

is negative semi-definite.

Let z be any vector, and define a quadratic form $Q_D = z'Dz$. Let $H = ((\partial^2/\partial x^2) L)$, and $H^{-1/2}$ be the symmetric negative square root of H^{-1}. Define

$$u = H^{-1/2} v \,, \quad \text{where} \quad v = -\frac{\partial}{\partial x} g \,, \quad \text{and} \quad y = H^{-1/2} z$$

Then,

$$Q_D = y'y - y'u(u'u)^{-1} u'y$$

$$= \|y\|^2 - \|u\|^{-2} \|u'y\|^2$$

By the Schwarz inequality, $Q_D \geq 0$.[22] So, $S(a, c)$ will be negative semi-definite if $(\partial^2/\partial x \partial a)L$ is positive semi-definite since under the conditions of the proposition $(\partial^2/\partial x \partial a)L$ is diagonal. But $(\partial^2/\partial x \partial a)L$ is positive semi-definite if $\gamma + \sum_{i=1}^{\infty} \lambda_i \delta^i \geq 0$. This completes the proof.

References

1. Arrow, K. J., E. W. Barankin, and D. Blackwell, "Admissible Points of Convex Sets", Contributions to the Theory of Games, V, II (Kuhn and Tucker, eds.), Princeton University Press, Princeton, 1953, pp. 87-92.

2. Arrow, K. J. and F. H. Hahn, General Competitive Analysis, Holden-Day, San Francisco, 1971.

3. Berger, M. S., "Generalized Differentiation and Utility Functionals for Commodity Spaces of Arbitrary Dimensions", in Preferences, Utility and Demand (J. Chipman, L. Hurwicz, M. Richter, and H. Sonnenschein, eds.), Harcourt, Brace Jovanovich, Inc., 1971.

4. Chichilnisky, G., "Nonlinear Functional Analysis and Optimal Economic Growth", forthcoming, Journal of Mathematical Analysis and Applications.

5. Chichilnisky, G. and P. J. Kalman, "An Application of Functional Analysis to Models of Efficient Allocation of Economic Resources", Working Paper, Harvard University, 1976.

6. Chichilnisky, G. and P. J. Kalman, "Properties of Critical Points and Operators in Economics", Journal of Mathematical Analysis and Applications, Feb. 1977.

7. Court, L., "Enterpreneurial and Consumer Demand Theories for Commodity Spectra, Part I and II", Econometrica, 9, April, July-October, 1941, pp. 241-297.

8. Dunford and Schwartz, Linear Operators, Interscience Publishers, New York, 1966.

9. Kalman, P., "Theory of Consumer Behavior when Prices Enter the Utility Function", Econometrica, Oct. 1968.

10. Kalman, P. and M. Intriligator, "Generalized Comparative Statics with Applications to Consumer Theory and Producer Theory", International Economic Review, 14, June 1973.

11. Kantorovich, L. V. and G. P. Akilov, Functional Analysis in Normed Spaces, Pergamon Press, MacMillan Co., N. Y., 1964.

12. Lang, S., Differential Manifolds, Addison-Wesley Series in Mathematics, 1972.

13. Luenberger, D. G., Optimization by Vector Space Methods, Wiley, 1969.

14. Riesz, F. and B. Sz-Nagy, Functional Analysis, Frederick Unger, New York, 1955.

15. Samuelson, P.A., Foundations of Economic Analysis, Cambridge, Mass., Harvard University Press, 1947.

16. Smale, S., "An Infinite Dimensional Version of Sard's Theorem", Amer. J. Math., 87 (1965), 861-866.

Applications of Thom's Transversality Theory and Brouwer Degree Theory to Economics*

by

Peter J. Kalman and Kuan-Pin Lin
SUNY at Stoney Brook and
Harvard University

August 1976
(revised May 1977)

I. Introduction

Recently, techniques of differential topology and global analysis were introduced into the economics literature by Debreu [6] and Smale [20], [21]. The tools of differential topology enables us to investigate the local uniqueness and continuity of the economic equilibria as well as the existence problem. The existence problem has been extensively studied during the last 20 years (see Arrow and Hahn [2] for a comprehensive survey). The mathematical tools for the solution were provided by algebraic topology in the form of fixed point theorems. In this differential framework, one can also show that the equilibrium varies in a continuous and unique manner with respect to changes in the economic data of the model. Debreu [6] investigated these equilibrium properties for classical pure exchange economies with a finite number of agents

*This work was supported in part by NSF grant GS-18174 and in part by the Urban Institute, Washington, D.C. P. J. Kalman is visiting Harvard from SUNY at Stony Brook. We thank K. J. Arrow, M. Hirsch, G. Laroque, H. Wiesmeth and J. Wolf for helpful comments.

and a finite number of consumption goods. His analysis is restricted to finite dimensional spaces in the sense that an economy is specified by a point of finite dimensional commodity space. Smale [20] extended this finite dimensional case to the case of allowing each agent's utility function to vary arbitrarily for the same type model as Debreu [6].

In this paper we consider an economic equilibrium model with externalities where each agent's utility function depends on the state of the economy which is specified by the allocations of each agent and also on a price system. This includes, as a special case, the Veblen-Scitovsky price influenced equilibrium models studied recently by Arrow and Hahn [2] and Kalman and Lin [11]. McKenzie [13] was the first to prove explicitly the existence of equilibrium where each consumer's preferences and each firm's production depends on the allocation of resources among other consumers and firms. However, this did not include price influenced economies. Arrow and Hahn [2] and Laffont and Laroque [12] also study the existence of equilibrium for a McKenzie type model. More recently, in the economics literature, Mas-Collel [15] and Shafer and Sonnenschein [19] prove the existence of pure exchange equilibrium with externalities without requiring complete or transitive preferences. Mantel [14] applies the same idea to a model with the presence of a complex tax structure and public goods.

Our approach, which differs from those of the above works on externalities, uses tools of differential topology to study the structure of the equilibria set. In particular, in addition to proving existence of equilibrium with externalities under certain assumptions (as in [13], [2], [12], [15], [19]), we also obtain local uniqueness and continuity of this equilibrium which are new results. In other words, under certain assumptions for "almost all" economies with externalities, there exists a finite number of equilibria which are stable.[1]

Section II presents the basic model. In Section III we prove local uniqueness of equilibria for "almost all" economies using transversality theory [1] of differential topology without requiring any convexity assumptions on preferences. We also obtain continuity of equilibria with respect to the economic data of the model. Finally, in Section IV we prove existence of equilibrium for this model using degree theory [16] of differential topology.

---

[1] Recently, Fuchs and Laroque [8] obtained local uniqueness and stability of equilibria for a McKenzie type model using a demand function approach. We study utility functions directly and do not require well defined demand functions and our methods of proofs differ.

II. The Model

We consider a space of economies with ℓ commodities and n agents. Let $P \doteq \{z \in R^{\ell} : z_i > 0, \; i = 1, \ldots, \ell\}$ be the commodity space where $x^h \in P$ is the consumption bundle of agent h $(h = 1, \ldots, n)$. Let $S = \{p \in P : \Sigma_{i=1}^{\ell} p_i = 1\}$ be the price space.

A state of an economy is a pair $(x, p) \in P^n \times S$ where $x = (x^1, \ldots, x^n)$. We denote the product space $P^n \times S$ as the state space. For each agent h, x^h is the choice variable and $(\tilde{x}^h, p) = (x^1, \ldots, x^{h-1}, x^{h+1}, \ldots, x^n, p) \in P^{n-1} \times S$ is the parameter vector which influences his/her decision making. The preferences of agent h can be represented by a real-valued function defined on the state space, i.e., $u^h : P^n \times S \to R$. In other words, we allow the preference of each agent to depend not only on his own consumptions but also on the consumptions of others and the price systems. We assume $u^h \in C^1(P^n \times S, R)$ and for every parameter vector $(\tilde{x}^h, p) \in P^{n-1} \times S$, $u^h(\cdot, \tilde{x}^h, p) \in C^2(P, R)$.[2] For a given parameter vector $(\tilde{x}^h, p)$, we assume further that $u^h(\cdot, \tilde{x}^h, p)$ fulfills a Debreu type boundary condition (for instance, see [7]) and $u^h(\cdot, \tilde{x}^h, p)$ satisfies a monotonicity assumption independent of the parameters $(\tilde{x}^h, p)$. We let $\bar{x}^h \in P$ be the resource endowment of agent h. Denote $u = (u^1, \ldots, u^n)$ and $\bar{x} = (\bar{x}^1, \ldots, \bar{x}^n) \in P^n$. An economy E is a list of utility functions (which depend on the state) and resource endowments i.e., $E = (u, \bar{x})$. Formally, we assume that each agent h in the economy E satisfies

A. 1. (Boundary Condition) For any parameter vector $(\tilde{x}^h, p) \in P^{n-1} \times S$, $u^h(\cdot, \tilde{x}^h, p)^{-1}(c) \subset P$ for every $c \in R$, and

---

[2] $C^k(X, Y)$ denotes the space of k times continuously differentiable functions from a topological space X to a topological space Y.

A. 2. (Monotonicity) $D_h u^h(x, p) \in P$ where $D_h u^h(x, p)$ is the derivative with respect to the h-th coordinate of vector x.[3]

Let $\mathcal{U} = \mathcal{U}(P^n \times S, R) = \{u^h \in C^1(P^n \times S, R): u^h(\cdot, \tilde{x}^h, p) \in C^2(P, R)$ for every $(\tilde{x}^h, p)$, and satisfies (A. 1), (A. 2)$\}$. $\mathcal{U}$ is called the space of utility functions for every agent h. For a special case of $\mathcal{U}$, we also consider a subspace of utility functions which possess a convexity property with respect to an agent's own consumptions, i. e.,

$$\mathcal{U}_0 = \left\{ u^h \in \mathcal{U}(P^n \times S, R) : D_h^2 u^h(x, p) | \{v \in R^\ell : v \cdot D_h u^h(x, p) = 0\} \text{ is negative definite for each } (x, p) \in P^n \times S \right\},$$

where $D_h^2 u^h(x, p)$ is a bilinear symmetric form of $u^h(x, p)$ with respect to x^h. Since the endowment as well as its distribution of each agent are also allowed to vary in the commodity space P, the economic characteristics of our model are completely specified by the product space $(\mathcal{U} \times P)^n$. Let $\mathcal{E} = (\mathcal{U} \times P)^n$ be the space of economies and an economy $E = (u, \bar{x}) \in \mathcal{E}$. In particular, $\mathcal{E}_0 = (\mathcal{U}_0 \times P)^n$ is a space of convex economies. Clearly, $\mathcal{E}$ and $\mathcal{E}_0$ are infinite dimensional spaces. We shall consider two different topologies on $\mathcal{E}$ for different purposes. For dealing with "generic" properties as we do in the next section, the most useful topology on $\mathcal{E}$, which we call the "Whitney" topology is defined by the product of the induced Whitney C^1 topology

---

[3] $\overline{u^h(\cdot, \tilde{x}^h, p)^{-1}(c)}$ means the closure of the indifference surface $u^h(\cdot, \tilde{x}^h, p)^{-1}(c)$ in P. Loosely speaking, A. 1 states that the indifference surfaces never intersect the boundary of commodity space and A. 2 claims that every commodity is desired by every agent for any parameter vector.

on $\mathcal{U}^n$ and the induced usual topology on P^n, provided the space $C^2(P, R)$ is endowed with the Whitney C^2 topology. Toward proving the existence theorem, the "compact-open" topology on $\mathscr{E}$ is then defined by replacing the Whitney C^1 topology and Whitney C^2 topology by the C^1 compact-open topology and the C^2 compact-open topology on $C^1(P^n \times S, R)$ and $C^2(P, R)$, respectively.[4]

For any economy $E = (u, \bar{x}) \in \mathscr{E}$, the budget set of agent h at a prevailing price system $p \in S$ is denoted as usual by $B^h(p, \bar{x}^h) = \{x^h \in P : p \cdot x^h = p \cdot \bar{x}^h\}$. Now we are in a position to define two concepts of equilibrium. For every economy $E \in \mathscr{E}$, a classical equilibrium is a state (x, p) with $\Sigma_{h=1}^n x^h = \Sigma_{h=1}^n \bar{x}^h$ and x^h is a maximal point of $u^h(\cdot, \tilde{x}^h, p)$ restricted to the budget set $B^h(p, \bar{x}^h)$ for every h. Given $(\tilde{x}^h, p)$, a maximal point of $u^h(\cdot, \tilde{x}^h, p)$ restricted to $B^h(p, \bar{x}^h)$ is also a critical point[5] of it. For a given parameter vector $(\tilde{x}^h, p)$, the condition for x^h to be a critical point of $u^h(\cdot, \tilde{x}^h, p)$ restricted to $B^h(p, \bar{x}^h)$ can be written as $D_h u^h(x, p) = \lambda^h p$ where λ^h is the Lagrangian multiplier of h. To avoid λ^h in the model, we substitute $\lambda^h = |D_h u^h(x, p)|$ where

$$|D_h u^h(x, p)| = \sum_{i=1}^{\ell} \frac{\partial u^h}{\partial x_i^h}(x, p) .$$

It is obvious that $\lambda^h > 0$ by A. 2. We formally define the set of

---

[4] For a definition of Whitney C^k topology and C^k compact-open topology on $C^k(X, Y)$, see Hirsch [9] and Smale [20].

[5] If $f: X \to Y$ is class C^1, a point $x \in X$ is a regular point of f if $Df(x): T_x X \to T_y Y$ is surjective with $y = f(x)$ where $Df(x)$ represents the derivative of the map f computed at x, which is a linear map from the tangent space of X at x to the tangent space of Y at y, denoted by $T_x X$ and $T_y Y$, respectively. If $Df(x)$ is not surjective, x is a critical point of f. y is called a regular value if every $x \in f^{-1}(y)$ is a regular point. y is a critical value if at least one $x \in f^{-1}(y)$ is a critical point.

<u>classical equilibria</u> for $E \in \mathcal{E}$ as

$$W(E) = \left\{(x,p) \in P^n \times S:\ u^h(x,p) \text{ is maximized},\ px^h = p\bar{x}^h,\ h = 1,\dots,n, \text{ and } \sum_{h=1}^n x^h = \sum_{h=1}^n \bar{x}^h\right\},$$

and the set of <u>extended equilibria</u>[6] for $E \in \mathcal{E}$ as

$$\Phi(E) = \left\{(x,p) \in P^n \times S:\ D_h u^h(x,p) = |D_h u^h(x,p)| \cdot p,\ px^h = p\bar{x}^h,\ h = 1,\dots,n, \text{ and } \sum_{h=1}^n x^h = \sum_{h=1}^n \bar{x}^h\right\}$$

Since the condition $px^n = p\bar{x}^n$ can be obtained from $px^h = p\bar{x}^h$, $h = 1,\dots,n-1$, and $\Sigma_{h=1}^n x^h = \Sigma_{h=1}^n \bar{x}^h$, the set of extended equilibria for every $E \in \mathcal{E}$ can be rewritten as

$$\Phi(E) = \left\{(x,p) \in P^n \times S:\ D_h u^h(x,p) = |D_h u^h(x,p)| \cdot p,\ h = 1,\dots,n,\ px^h = p\bar{x}^h,\ h = 1,\dots,n-1, \text{ and } \sum_{h=1}^n x^h = \sum_{h=1}^n \bar{x}^h\right\}.$$

For every economy $E = (u,\bar{x}) \in \mathcal{E}$, we define a map $\psi_E: P^n \times S \to I^n \times R^{n+\ell-1}$ by

$$\psi_E(x,p) = \left(D_h u^h(x,p) - |D_h u^h(x,p)| \cdot p,\ h = 1,\dots,n;\ p\bar{x}^h - px^h,\ h = 1,\dots,n-1;\ \sum_{h=1}^n \bar{x}^h - \sum_{h=1}^n x^h\right)$$

where $I = \left\{z \in R^\ell:\ \sum_{i=1}^{\ell} z_i = 0\right\}$

[6] This concept was first used by Smale in [20] for a different model. From an economic viewpoint, this concept is of little interest. However, it is useful since it can be used as a tool to derive economically interesting results for properties of classical equilibria.

Obviously, $\psi_E \in C^1(P^n \times S, I^n \times R^{n+\ell-1})$ since for every h, $u^h \in C^1(P^n \times S, R)$ and $u^h(\cdot, \tilde{x}^h, p) \in C^2(P, R)$ for every $(\tilde{x}^h, p)$. By definition of $\Phi(E)$, we have $\Phi(E) = \psi_E^{-1}(0)$ and $W(E) \subset \psi_E^{-1}(0)$ for every $E \in \mathscr{E}$. That is, if (x, p) is a classical equilibrium, it is an extended equilibrium, and the C^1 map ψ_E vanishes at (x, p). It is clear that $W(E) = \psi_E^{-1}(0)$ for every convex economy, i. e., $E \in \mathscr{E}_0$. Furthermore, $\Phi(E)$ is closed in $P^n \times S$ since $\Phi(E) = \psi_E^{-1}(0)$ and ψ_E is C^1. By the boundary condition A. 1 and monotonicity assumption A. 2, we have the following

PROPOSITION 1. $\Phi(E)$ _is a compact subset in_ $P^n \times S$ _for every_ $E \in \mathscr{E}$.

III. Local Uniqueness and Continuity of Equilibria

In this section we prove local uniqueness and continuity of extended and classical equilibria for "almost all" economies in $\mathscr{E}$, which is defined by a transversality condition on ψ_E below. Actually, we apply the concept of transversality only in the very special sense. That is, $f \in C^1(X, Y)$ is transversal to y denoted $f \pitchfork y$ if either $y \neq f(x)$ for all x or $Df(x)[T_x X] = T_y Y$ for all $x \in f^{-1}(y)$, which is to say that y is a regular value of f. In fact, f is regular if and only if $f \pitchfork y$ for every $y \in Y$. We need a few more definitions. An element $E \in \mathscr{E}$ is called a _regular economy_ if and only if the associated map ψ_E is transversal to the origin, i. e.,

$\psi_E \pitchfork 0$. Moreover, the space of regular economies is denoted by the set $\mathscr{R} = \{E \in \mathscr{E} : \psi_E \pitchfork 0\}$ and the space of convex regular economies is $\mathscr{R}_0 = \mathscr{R} \cap \mathscr{E}_0$. By a theorem of differential topology (for instance, [1], p. 45), $\psi_E^{-1}(0) = \Phi(E)$ is a C^1 submanifold of $P^n \times S$ for every $E \in \mathscr{R}$. In view of the space of economies $\mathscr{E}$, we have

PROPOSITION 2. *$\mathscr{R}$ is open and dense in $\mathscr{E}$ with respect to the "Whitney" topology defined on $\mathscr{E}$.*[7]

Proof. Since P and S are locally compact, we let $\{K_\alpha\}$ and $\{L_\alpha\}$ be the sequences of compact subsets in P and S respectively, such that $K_\alpha \subset K_{\alpha+1}$, $L_\alpha \subset L_{\alpha+1}$ and $P = \cup K_\alpha$, $S = \cup L_\alpha$. For each $u^h \in C^1(P^n \times S, R)$, let $u^h_\alpha = u^h | K^n_\alpha \times L_\alpha \in C^1(K^n_\alpha \times L_\alpha, R)$. The spaces $C^1(K^n_\alpha \times L_\alpha, R)$ are Banach spaces (see [1], p. 24). Moreover, they are metrizable and separable, hence they are second countable. It is easy to see that the space $C^1(P^n \times S, R)$ is the inverse limit[8] of the sequence $\{C^1(K^n_\alpha \times L_\alpha, R), f_\alpha\}$. That is,

---

[7] The density and openness of $\mathscr{R}$ in $\mathscr{E}$ implies that any economy can be approximated by a regular economy and any regular economy is still regular under small perturbations of economic data in the model.

[8] Let X_α be a topological space and f_α be a continuous map from X_α into $X_{\alpha-1}$, for each α. The sequence $\{X_\alpha, f_\alpha\}$ is called an inverse limit sequence. The inverse limit space of the sequence $\{X_\alpha, f_\alpha\}$ is the following subset of $\Pi_\alpha X_\alpha$: $X = \{x \in \Pi_\alpha X_\alpha : f_\alpha(x_\alpha) = x_{\alpha-1}$ for each α and $x_\alpha \in X_\alpha$, $x_{\alpha-1} \in X_{\alpha-1}\}$ (see [23] for its formal definition and properties).

$$f_\alpha : C^1(K_\alpha^n \times L_\alpha, R) \to C^1(K_{\alpha-1}^n \times L_{\alpha-1}, R)$$

defined by $f_\alpha(u_\alpha^h) = u_{\alpha-1}^h = u_\alpha^h | K_{\alpha-1}^n \times L_{\alpha-1}$ is clearly continuous. Define $\mathscr{U}_\alpha = \{u_\alpha^h \in C^1(K_\alpha^n \times L_\alpha, R) : u_\alpha^h(\cdot, x^h, p) \in C^2(K_\alpha, R)$ for every (x^h, p), and A. 1, A. 2 are satisfied$\}$, and $\mathscr{E}_\alpha = (\mathscr{U}_\alpha \times P)^n$. Then $\mathscr{U}$ and $\mathscr{E}$ are the inverse limit spaces of the sequences $\{\mathscr{U}_\alpha, f'_\alpha\}$ and $\{\mathscr{E}_\alpha, g_\alpha\}$ respectively, where $f'_\alpha = f_\alpha | \mathscr{U}_\alpha$, $g_\alpha : \mathscr{E}_\alpha \to \mathscr{E}_{\alpha-1}$ defined by

$$g_\alpha = (\underbrace{f'_\alpha, \ldots, f'_\alpha}_{n \text{ times}}, \text{id})$$

and id, the identity map, from P^n to P^n. Clearly, $\mathscr{E}_\alpha$ is a C^1 (Banach) manifold and second countable. Define the sequence $\{\mathscr{R}_\alpha, g'_\alpha\}$ as $\mathscr{R}_\alpha = \{E_\alpha \in \mathscr{E}_\alpha : \psi_{E_\alpha} \pitchfork 0\}$, $g'_\alpha = g_\alpha | \mathscr{R}_\alpha$ and $\psi_{E_\alpha} = \psi_E | K_\alpha^n \times L_\alpha$. Then $\mathscr{R}$ is the inverse limit of $\{\mathscr{R}_\alpha, g'_\alpha\}$.

We now claim that $\mathscr{R}_\alpha$ is open and dense in $\mathscr{E}_\alpha$ for each α. We apply the Transversal Density Theorem 19. 1 of [1], p. 48. Conditions (1), (2) and (3) of 19. 1 are satisfied. We need to check condition (4) of Theorem 19. 1 of [1]. First, let $\psi_\alpha : \mathscr{E}_\alpha \times K_\alpha^n \times L_\alpha \to I^n \times R^{n+\ell-1}$ defined by $\psi_\alpha(E_\alpha, x, p) = \psi_{E_\alpha}(x, p)$ for each $E_\alpha \in \mathscr{E}_\alpha$ and $(x, p) \in K_\alpha^n \times L_\alpha$ be the evaluation map of ψ_{E_α}. It is clear that ψ_α is C^1 (for instance, see [1], p. 25). We go on to prove that $\psi_\alpha \pitchfork 0$. By definition, $\psi_\alpha : \mathscr{E}_\alpha \times K_\alpha^n \times L_\alpha \to I^n \times R^{n+\ell-1}$ is given by

$$\psi_a(E_a, x, p) = \Big(D_h u_a^h(x,p) - |D_h u_a^h(x,p)| \cdot p, \quad h = 1, \ldots, n; \; p\bar{x}^h - px^h,$$

$$h = 1, \ldots, n-1; \; \sum_{h=1}^{n} \bar{x}^h - \sum_{h=1}^{n} x^h \Big) .$$

Its derivative

$$D\psi_a(E_a, x, p) : T_{(E_a, x, p)}(\mathscr{E}_a \times K_a^n \times L_a) \to T_{\psi_a(E_a, x, p)}(I^n \times R^{n+\ell-1})$$

at (E_a, x, p) is defined by

$$D\psi_a(E_a, x, p)(\dot{E}_a, \dot{x}, \dot{p}) = \Bigg(\frac{\partial^2 u_a^h}{\partial x_r^h \partial E_a} E_a - \sum_{i=1}^{\ell} \frac{\partial^2 u_a^h}{\partial x_i^h \partial E_a} p_r \dot{E}_a$$

$$+ \sum_{k=1}^{n} \sum_{j=1}^{\ell} \frac{\partial^2 u_a^h}{\partial x_r^h \partial x_j^k} \dot{x}_j^k - \sum_{k=1}^{n} \sum_{j=1}^{\ell} \sum_{i=1}^{\ell} \frac{\partial^2 u_a^h}{\partial x_i^h \partial x_j^k} p_r \dot{x}_j^k$$

$$+ \sum_{j=1}^{\ell} \frac{\partial^2 u_a^h}{\partial x_r^h \partial p_j} \dot{p}_j - \sum_{j=1}^{\ell} \sum_{i=1}^{\ell} \frac{\partial^2 u_a^h}{\partial x_i^h \partial p_j} p_r \dot{p}_j$$

$$- \sum_{i=1}^{\ell} \frac{\partial u_a^h}{\partial x_i^h} \dot{p}_r , \qquad r = 1, \ldots, \ell, \quad h = 1, \ldots, n ,$$

$$\dot{p}(\bar{x}^h - x^h) + p(\dot{\bar{x}}^h - \dot{x}^h), \quad h = 1, \ldots, n-1; \; \sum_{h=1}^{n} \dot{\bar{x}}^h - \sum_{h=1}^{n} \dot{x}^h \Bigg)$$

where

$$(\dot{E}_a, \dot{x}, \dot{p}) \in T_{(E_a, x, p)}(\mathscr{E}_a \times K_a^n \times L_a)$$

and $\dot{E}_a = (\dot{u}_a, \dot{\bar{x}})$. Without loss of generality, we take $\dot{E}_a = (0, \dot{\bar{x}})$ and $\dot{x} = 0$, then

$$D\psi_a(E_a, x, p)((0,\dot{x}), 0, \dot{p}) = \Bigg(\sum_{j=1}^{\ell} \frac{\partial^2 u_a^h}{\partial x_r^h \partial p_j} \dot{p}_j - \sum_{j=1}^{\ell} \sum_{i=1}^{\ell} \frac{\partial^2 u_a^h}{\partial x_i^h \partial p_j} p_r \dot{p}_j$$

$$- \sum_{i=1}^{\ell} \frac{\partial u_a^h}{\partial x_i^h} \dot{p}_r , \quad r = 1, \ldots, \ell, \quad h = 1, \ldots, n;$$

$$\dot{p}(\bar{x}^h - x^h) + p\dot{\bar{x}}^h, \quad h = 1, \ldots, n-1; \quad \sum_{h=1}^{n} \dot{\bar{x}}^h \Bigg)$$

For each $(a, b, c) \in T_{\psi_a(E_a, x, p)}(I^n \times R^{n+\ell-1})$ with $a = (a^1, \ldots, a^n) \in T_{\psi_a(E_a, x, p)}(I^n)$, $b = (b^1, \ldots, b^{n-1}) \in R^{n-1}$ and $c = (c_1, \ldots, c_\ell) \in R^\ell$, there exists $((0,\dot{x}), 0, \dot{p}) \in T_{(E_a, x, p)}(\mathscr{E}_a \times K_a^n \times L_a)$ such that $D\psi_a(E_a, x, p)((0,\dot{x}); 0, \dot{p}) = (a, b, c)$ since

$$\sum_{k=1}^{\ell} a_k^h = 0 , \qquad \sum_{i=1}^{\ell} \frac{\partial u_a^h}{\partial x_i^h} > 0$$

for each h and $p \neq 0$. Therefore $D\psi_a(E_a, x, p)$ is surjective on $T_{\psi_a(E_a, x, p)}(I^n \times R^{n+\ell-1})$. In particular, $\psi \pitchfork 0$. This shows that condition (4) of the Transversal Density Theorem 19.1 of [1] is satisfied. Hence $\mathscr{R}_a$ is dense in $\mathscr{E}_a$. The openness of $\mathscr{R}_a$ in $\mathscr{E}_a$ follows from the Openness of Transversal Intersection Theorem 18.2 o [1], p. 47.

Let $r_\alpha : \mathscr{E} \to \mathscr{E}_\alpha$ for every α be the canonical restriction maps. To prove that $\mathscr{R}$ is open and dense in $\mathscr{E}$ with respect to the "Whitney" topology, we first claim that $r_\alpha^{-1}(\mathscr{R}_\alpha)$ is dense in $\mathscr{E}$ with respect to the "Whitney" topology. We note that r_α is not an open map with respect to the "Whitney" topology on $\mathscr{E}$. But in fact, we do not need the openness of r_α, and it would suffice if we know that the image of an open set of $\mathscr{E}$ under r_α contains an open set of $\mathscr{E}_\alpha$. Let $N(E) = N^\epsilon(u) \times N(\bar{x})$ be a neighborhood of $E = (u, \bar{x})$ in $\mathscr{E}$ with respect to the "Whitney" topology, where $N(\bar{x})$ is an usual neighborhood of $\bar{x}$ in P and $N^\epsilon(u) = \{u' \in \mathscr{U}^n : \| D^k u^h(x, p) - D^k u^{h'}(x, p)\| < \epsilon^h(x, p)$ for all $(x, p) \in P^n \times S$, $k = 0, 1$ and $h = 1, \ldots, n\}$ with $\epsilon^h : P^n \times S \to R$ being a positive continuous function for each h. As we discuss earlier, $r_\alpha(N(E)) \subset \mathscr{E}_\alpha$ is not an open set in general. However, if we shrink $N(E)$ to a neighborhood $N^*(E) = N^\delta(u) \times N(\bar{x})$ with $\delta^h \le \epsilon^h$ and $\delta^h : P^n \times S \to R$ is a positive continuous function and increasing with respect to $x^h \in P$ for every h, it is obvious that for every $E'_\alpha = (u'_\alpha, \bar{x}') \in N^*_\alpha(E_\alpha) = N^\delta_\alpha(u_\alpha) \times N(\bar{x})$, $u^{h'}_\alpha$ can be extended to a function $u^{h'} \in \mathscr{U}$ with $u^{h'}_\alpha = u^{h'} | K^n_\alpha \times L_\alpha$ for every h, where $N^\delta_\alpha(u_\alpha) = \{u'_\alpha \in \mathscr{U}^n_\alpha : \| D^k u^h_\alpha(x, p) - D^k u^{h'}_\alpha(x, p)\| < \delta^h(x, p)$ for every $(x, p) \in K^n_\alpha \times L_\alpha$, $k = 0, 1$, and $h = 1, \ldots, n\}$. Hence $r_\alpha(N^*(E)) = N^*_\alpha(E_\alpha)$ is open in $\mathscr{E}_\alpha$ and consequently $r_\alpha(N(E))$ contains an open set. Together with the fact that $\mathscr{R}_\alpha$ is dense in $\mathscr{E}_\alpha$, we have $r_\alpha(N(E)) \cap \mathscr{R}_\alpha \ne \phi$. This means that there exists an $E' \in N(E)$ such that $r_\alpha(E') \in \mathscr{R}_\alpha$ or $E' \in r_\alpha^{-1}(\mathscr{R}_\alpha)$. Hence $N(E) \cap r_\alpha^{-1}(\mathscr{R}_\alpha) \ne \phi$, or equivalently $r_\alpha^{-1}(\mathscr{R}_\alpha)$ is dense in $\mathscr{E}$. By definition, $\mathscr{R} = \cap_\alpha r_\alpha^{-1}(\mathscr{R}_\alpha)$. Therefore, $\mathscr{R}$ is dense in $\mathscr{E}$ with respect to the "Whitney" topology since $\mathscr{E}$ is a Baire space. Moreover, if $E \in \mathscr{R}$, then by definition, $E_\alpha \in \mathscr{R}_\alpha$ with $g'_\alpha(E_\alpha) = E_{\alpha-1}$ for each α. Since $\mathscr{R}_\alpha$ is open in $\mathscr{E}_\alpha$, there exists a neighborhood $N_\alpha(E_\alpha) = N^\epsilon_\alpha(u_\alpha) \times N(\bar{x})$ of E_α in $\mathscr{E}_\alpha$ with $N_\alpha(E_\alpha) \subset \mathscr{R}_\alpha$ for each α. In particular, $N_\alpha^\epsilon(u_\alpha) = \{u'_\alpha \in \mathscr{U}_\alpha^n : \|D^k u_\alpha^h(x, p) - D^k u_\alpha^{h'}(x, p)\| < \epsilon_\alpha^h(x, p)$ for every $(x, p) \in K_\alpha^n \times L_\alpha$, $k = 0, 1$ and $h = 1, \ldots, n\}$, where $\epsilon_\alpha^h : K_\alpha^n \times L_\alpha \to R$ is a positive continuous function for every h. We now choose a positive continuous function $\delta^h : P^n \times S \to R$ with $\delta^h(x, p) \leq \epsilon_\alpha^h(x, p)$ for every $(x, p) \in K_\alpha^n \times L_\alpha$ and all α. Then $N^*(E) = N^\delta(u) \times N(\bar{x})$ is a neighborhood of E in $\mathscr{E}$ and $N^*(E) \subset \mathscr{R}$. Hence the openness of $\mathscr{R}$ in $\mathscr{E}$ follows with respect to the "Whitney" topology. Q.E.D.

For every regular economy $E \in \mathscr{R}$, we have $\psi_E \pitchfork 0$. By the openness property of $\mathscr{R}$, $\psi_{E'} \pitchfork 0$ for $E' \in \mathscr{R}$ sufficiently near E. One might expect that for E' near E, $\psi_{E'}^{-1}(0)$ and $\psi_E^{-1}(0)$ are close to each other. In other words, we have

THEOREM 1. <u>The extended equilibrium correspondence</u> Φ <u>defined by</u> $\Phi(E) = \psi_E^{-1}(0)$ for every $E \in \mathscr{R}$ <u>is continuous, i.e., it is stable for every</u> $E \in \mathscr{R}$, <u>with respect to the "Whitney" topology</u>.

<u>Proof</u>: We know that ψ_α is C^1. Moreover, for every $E_\alpha \in \mathscr{R}_\alpha$, ψ_{E_α} is a C^1 local diffeomorphism by the inverse function theorem since $D\psi_{E_\alpha}(x, p) : T_{(x,p)}(K_\alpha^n \times L_\alpha) \to T_{\psi_{E_\alpha}(x,p)}(I^n \times R^{n+\ell-1})$ with $(x, p) \in \psi_{E_\alpha}^{-1}(0)$ is an isomorphism (see [16]). Hence, the stability property of the map $\Phi_\alpha = \Phi|\mathscr{R}_\alpha \to P^n \times S$ follows from an application of the implicit function theorem on the evaluation map ψ_α. That is, there exist neighborhoods $N_\alpha(E_\alpha)$ of $E_\alpha \in \mathscr{R}_\alpha$ and V of $(x, p) \in K_\alpha^n \times L_\alpha \subset P^n \times S$, and a C^1 function $\xi_\alpha : N_\alpha(E_\alpha) \to V$ such that

$\psi_a(E'_a, \xi_a(E'_a)) = 0$ for every $E'_a \in N_a(E_a)$ and $\xi_a(E_a) = (x, p)$. Since $\Phi_{a-1}(E_{a-1}) \subset \Phi_a(E_a)$ for every a, we have the following diagram

$$\begin{array}{ccc} N_{a-1}(E_{a-1}) & \xleftarrow{\ g'_a \mid N_a(E_a)\ } & N_a(E_a) \\ \downarrow \xi_{a-1} & & \downarrow \xi_a \\ V & \xleftarrow{\ \text{id}\ } & V \end{array}$$

which is commutative, i.e., $\xi_{a-1} \circ g'_a | N_a(E_a) = \text{id} \circ \xi_a$ for every a. This implies that for each $E \in \mathscr{R}$ there is a continuous function $\xi : N^*(E) \to V$ such that $\psi(E', \xi(E')) = 0$ for every $E' \in N^*(E)$ and $\xi(E) = (x, p)$, where $N^*(E)$ is a neighborhood as described in the proof of Proposition 2. Hence the extended equilibrium correspondence Φ is stable for every $E \in \mathscr{R}$ with respect to the "Whitney" topology. Q. E. D.

COROLLARY 1. *The classical equilibrium correspondence defined on the space of convex regular economies is continuous. That is,* $W(E)$ *is stable for every* $E \in \mathscr{R}_0$ *with respect to the "Whitney" topology.*

As an application of Theorem 1 and Corollary 1, we note that the space of exchange economies without externalities described in [20] appears as a subset of $\mathscr{E}$, the space of economies with externalities. That is, let $\mathscr{E}_1$ denote the space of economies without external effects, so $\mathscr{E}_1 \subset \mathscr{E}$ since utility functions for every agent h, $u^h : P^n \times S \to R$ are constant along $P^{n-1} \times S$. Given $E \in \mathscr{R}_1 \subset \mathscr{E}_1$, a regular economy without external effects, and a family of regular economies with externalities $\{E^q\}$ such that E^q converges to E, we have by continuity or stability of Φ defined on $\mathscr{R}$, $\Phi(E^q)$ converges to $\Phi(E)$

continuously, which is the equilibrium set of an exchange economy without external effects. This asserts the continuity of extended equilibria for economies with vanishing external effects. By the same argument applied on W, one gets the continuity of classical equilibria for convex economies with vanishing external effects (see [8] and compare).

Next, we prove local uniqueness of the equilibria for an open and dense subset $\mathcal{R}$ of the space of all economies $\mathcal{E}$ with respect to the "Whitney" topology.

THEOREM 2. For every regular economy $E = (u, \bar{x}) \in \mathcal{R}$, the extended equilibrium set $\Phi(E)$ is a finite set.

Proof: Since $\Phi(E) = \psi_E^{-1}(0)$ is compact for every $E \in \mathcal{E}$ by Proposition 1, and $\psi_E^{-1}(0)$ is a submanifold with zero dimension if $E \in \mathcal{R}$, we have $\Phi(E)$ is a finite set. Q.E.D.

COROLLARY 2. For every regular economy $E \in \mathcal{R}$, the classical equilibrium set $W(E)$ is also a finite set.

REMARK 1. As in [20] the local uniqueness and stability of equilibria can be obtained under weaker conditions. In particular, there is no need to assume boundary condition A.1. Proposition 1 now is not true, but still $\Phi(E)$ is closed in $P^n \times S$. Hence, $\Phi(E)$ and $W(E)$ are locally unique for every $E \in \mathcal{R}$. In other words, for every $E \in \mathcal{R}$, $\Phi(E)$ and $W(E)$ are discrete sets in $P^n \times S$. Finiteness is a fairly strong conclusion which follows from a boundary condition imposed on the commodity space for every agent in the economy.

IV. Existence of Equilibrium

Although the number of extended or classical equilibria for every regular economy E is finite, it is possible that $\Phi(E)$ or $W(E)$ is an empty set. To show $\Phi(E) \neq \phi$ and $W(E) \neq \phi$, we first prove the following.

PROPOSITION 3. *There exists a regular convex economy which has unique equilibrium.*

Proof: We prove this proposition by considering a nonempty subset of $\mathcal{U}_0$ for each agent, which contains additive separable utility functions with respect to $x^1, \ldots, x^n$ and p, denoted by $\mathcal{U}_{S0} \subset \mathcal{U}_0 \subset \mathcal{U}$. Define $\mathcal{E}_{S0} = (\mathcal{U}_{S0} \times P)^n$, then $\mathcal{E}_{S0} \subset \mathcal{E}_0 \subset \mathcal{E}$. For an $E = (u, \bar{x}) \in \mathcal{E}_{S0}$, let $\bar{x}$ be an equilibrium allocation (this is possible if we choose $E = (u, \bar{x})$ with $u^1 = \cdots = u^n$, $\bar{x}^1 = \cdots = \bar{x}^n$). Then, by the continuous differentiability and monotonicity of u^h for every h, there exists a unique $p^* \in S$ such that $\psi_E(\bar{x}, p^*) = 0$. In particular,

$$D_h u^h(\bar{x}, p^*) = |D_h u^h(\bar{x}, p^*)| \cdot p^*$$

for every agent h. Since $u^h \in \mathcal{U}_{S0}$, by a well known result of consumer theory on convex preferences (for instance, see [17]), $p^* x^h > p^* \bar{x}^h$ for every h with $x^h \neq \bar{x}^h$ and $\psi_E(x, p^*) = 0$. This is a self-contradiction. Hence $(\bar{x}, p^*)$ is a unique equilibrium for E. Furthermore, the derivative matrix of ψ_E has rank $\ell n + \ell - 1$ at $(\bar{x}, p^*)$. This follows from the fact that for each agent h, $|D_h u^h(\bar{x}, p^*)| > 0$ and $D_h^2 u^h(\bar{x}, p^*)$ as a bilinear symmetric form on the space $\{v \in R^{\ell} : v \cdot D_h u^h(\bar{x}, p^*) = 0\}$ is negative definite. Hence $E = (u, \bar{x}) \in \mathscr{R}$. Q.E.D.

THEOREM 3. *There exists extended equilibrium for every economy, i.e.,* $\Phi(E) \neq \phi$ *for all* $E \in \mathscr{E}$.

Proof: First, we check $\mathscr{E}$ is arcwise connected. Let $E, E' \in \mathscr{E}$, we construct $E^t = tE + (1-t)E'$ for $t \in [0,1]$, i.e., $E^t = (u^t, \bar{x}^t) = (tu + (1-t)u', t\bar{x} + (1-t)\bar{x}')$. By the "compact-open" topology given on $\mathscr{E}$, $u^{ht} \in C^1(P^n \times S, R)$, $\bar{x}^{ht} \in P$ for every h. Moreover, u^{ht} satisfies A.1 and A.2. Thus $E^t = (u^t, \bar{x}^t) \in \mathscr{E}$.
From Proposition 1, we have the extended equilibrium manifold $\psi_E^{-1}(0)$ is compact in $P^n \times S$. Therefore, the Brouwer degree is defined (see [16]). If $E \in \mathscr{R}$, the degree of the map ψ_E is equal to the algebraic sum of the orientations (see [16]) of the elements of $\psi_E^{-1}(0)$. Let $\deg \psi_E$ denote the degree of map ψ_E. By Proposition 3, there exists $E \in \mathscr{R}_0 \subset \mathscr{E}$, $\deg \psi_E$ is one. Finally, the Brouwer degree is a homotopy invariant, so that $\deg \psi_E$ is one for every $E \in \mathscr{E}$. This implies that $\Phi(E) = \psi_E^{-1}(0) \neq \phi$ for every $E \in \mathscr{E}$. Q.E.D.

COROLLARY 3. *For every convex economy there is a classical equilibrium, i.e.,* $W(E) \neq \phi$ *for all* $E \in \mathscr{E}_0$.

Proof: It follows directly from $W(E) = \psi_E^{-1}(0)$ for every $E \in \mathscr{E}_0$. Q.E.D.

REMARK 2. It is obvious from the definition of Brouwer degree, $\Phi(E)$ and $W(E)$ have an odd number of elements for every $E \in \mathscr{R}$ and $E \in \mathscr{R}_0$, respectively. In particular, if the sign of the determinant of the non-singular matrix of the derivatives of ψ_E at (x, p) with rank $\ell n + \ell - 1$ were constant for every $(x, p) \in \psi_E^{-1}(0)$, there is only one extended or classical equilibrium for E in $\mathscr{E}$ or $\mathscr{E}_0$.

References

1. Abraham, R. and J. Robbin, Transversal Mappings and Flows, W. A. Benjamin, Inc., New York, 1967.

2. Arrow, K. J. and F. H. Hahn, General Competitive Analysis, Holden-Day, San Francisco, 1971.

3. Chichilnisky, G. and P. J. Kalman, "Comparative Statics of Less Neoclassical Agents", International Economic Review, forthcoming.

4. Chichilnisky, G. and P. J. Kalman, "Special Properties of Critical Points and Operators of Parametrized Manifolds in Economics," Journal of Mathematical Analysis and Applications, Feb. 1977.

5. Debreu, G., Theory of Value, J. W. Wiley, 1959.

6. Debreu, G., "Economies with a Finite Set of Equilibria", Econometrica 38, 1970, pp. 387-392.

7. Debreu, G., "Smooth Preferences", Econometrica 40, 1972, pp. 603-615.

8. Fuchs, G., and G. Larque, "Continuity of Equilibria for Economies with Vanishing External Effects," Journal of Economic Theory 9, 1974, pp. 1-22.

9. Hirsch, M. W., Differential Topology, Springer Verlag, New York, 1976.

10. Kalman, P. J., "Theory of Consumer Behavior when Prices Enter the Utility Function", Econometrica 36, 1968, pp. 497-510.

11. Kalman, P. J. and K.-P. Lin, "Equilibrium Theory in Veblen-Scitovsky Economies: Local Uniqueness, Stability and Existence", Working Paper, Harvard University, July, 1977.

12. Laffont, J. J., and G. Laroque, "Effects externes et théorie de l'équilibre général," Cahiers du Séminaire d'Econométrie, CNRS, 1972.

13. McKenzie, L. W., "Competitive Equilibrium with Dependent Consumer Preferences", in National Bureau of Standards and Department of the Air Force, "The Second Symposium on Linear Programming", Washington, D.C., 1955.

14. Mantel, R. R., "General Equilibrium and Optimal Taxes", Journal of Mathematical Economics 2, 1975, pp. 187-200.

15. Mas-Colell, A., "An Equilibrium Existence Theorem without Complete or Transitive Preferences", Journal of Mathematical Economics 1, 1974, pp. 237-246.

16. Milnor, J., Topology from a Differentiable Viewpoint, University of Virginia Press, 1965.

17. Samuelson, P. A., The Foundations of Economic Analysis, Harvard University Press, Cambridge, Mass., 1947.

18. Scitovsky, T., "Some Consequences of Habit of Judging Quality by Price", Review of Economic Studies 12, 1945, pp. 100-105.

19. Shafer, W. and H. Sonnenschein, "Some Theorems on the Existence of Competitive Equilibrium", Journal of Economic Theory, 11, 1975, pp. 83-93.

20. Smale, S., "Global Analysis and Economics IIA: Extensions of a Theorem of Debreu," Journal of Mathematical Economics 1, 1974, pp. 1-14.

21. Smale, S., "Global Analysis and Economics IV: Finiteness and Stability of Equilibria with General Consumption Sets and Production", Journal of Mathematical Economics 1, 1974, pp. 119-127.

22. Veblen, T., The Theory of the Leisure Class, Macmillan, New York, 1899.

23. Wallace, A. H., Algebraic Topology: Homology and Cohomology, Benjamin, N. Y., 1970.

Symbol	Description
$\in$	belongs to
Σ	capital sigma
$\frac{\partial}{\partial x}$, $\frac{\partial^2}{\partial x^2}$	partial derivatives
α	lower case alpha
β	lower case beta
λ	lower case lambda
ξ	lower case xi
Φ	capital phi
Ψ	capital psi
Π	capital pi
$\subset$	subset
$\pitchfork$	transversal intersection
$\mathscr{U}$	upper case script u
$\mathscr{E}$	upper case script e
$\mathscr{R}$	upper case script r

ILLUSION-FREE DEMAND BEHAVIOR IN A MONETARY ECONOMY: THE GENERAL CONDITIONS

by

Richard Dusansky and Peter J. Kalman
State University of New York and Stony Brook

In monetary models the link between micro-foundations and macro-analysis, as it relates to demand behavior that is free of money illusion, is less than straightforward. If one assumes that an individual agent maximizes the usual neoclassical-type utility function, which contains consumption commodities exclusively as arguments, then the resulting commodity demand functions are homogeneous of degree zero in prices, initial money holdings and income; aggregation problems aside, it is therefore not unreasonable to assume that the aggregate market demand curves also exhibit this property. However, if one focuses on a monetary economy, and allows real balances to *generally* enter the agent's objective function, then the resulting commodity demand functions are not homogeneous of degree zero; demand behavior does exhibit money illusion. In this type of monetary model, employed in various versions by Dusansky-Kalman and Grandmont, among others, the assumption of the absence of money illusion in aggregate demand behavior needs careful justification; it becomes necessary to impose further restrictions on the underlying micro-monetary framework. This paper reconsiders the microeconomic foundations of money illusion in a monetary neoclassical model which incorporates a generalized real balance effect into the utility function, and presents new results.

In undertaking the analysis, we maintain the standard focus on demand behavior, defining an individual to be free of money illusion "if the amount he demands of any real good remains invariant under any change which does not affect relative prices, the rate of interest, the time stream of incomes and the real value of initial bond and money holdings,"[1] and seek to find the weakest restrictions on individual behavior consistent with this homogeneity of degree zero demand property. Thus far the literature contains two alternative sufficiency conditions which effect this outcome. The first, well known for over thirty years, is that the utility function be homogeneous in money and prices. The second is that the marginal utility functions be homogeneous in money and prices (Dusansky-Kalman, 1974). This latter condition is less restrictive than the former, for it does not require that the utility function itself be homogeneous.[2] However, it does require that one make some kind of (albeit weaker) homogeneity assumptions in order to attain the homogeneity (of demand) result.

---

1 D. Patinkin (1965), p. 72 (and essentially repeated on p. 140). Similarly, but of earlier vintage, see Marschak (1943), p. 40.

2 The recent comments by Clower-Riley (1976) indicate that this distinction is not well understood and demonstrates that there exists some confusion about the relationship between homogeneity assumptions (as they relate to utility functions) and the homogeneity of demand result. They are distinctly different properties. In fact, there need be no relationship at all between the two; for the results in the current paper imply that one need make no homogeneity assumptions whatsoever in order to generate the absence of money illusion in demand property.

The present paper develops a new, more general condition for effecting the absence of money illusion result. This condition will exhibit several characteristics: First, homogeneity assumptions are unnecessary. There is no need for the utility function to be homogeneous or for the marginal utility functions to be homogeneous in any way; one thus no longer needs homogeneity assumptions to get homogeneity results. Second, the marginal rate of substitution between commodities need not be invariant under the money illusion disturbance. In a model with a general real balance effect, it is plausible that wider disparity in absolute prices, engendered by the money illusion experiment, can alter the individual's marginal rates of substitution, at the same time that his demand behavior is free of money illusion. This possible situation, precluded by the first two alternative conditions, is admissible under the new condition. As a result the theory now allows for more diverse economic behavior. The third characteristic is that the new condition constitutes the least restrictive condition that can be employed to generate the absence of money illusion result; it is proved that no weaker conditions are attainable.

We begin by deriving the most general condition under which the commodity demand functions in a neoclassical micro-monetary model are free of money illusion. We consider the general formulation of consumer utility maximization when real balances enter the utility function. Specifically, we consider the problem of maximizing a utility function of the form

(1) $$u = u(x_1,\ldots,x_n,P)$$

where $x_1,\ldots,x_{n-1}$ represents the week's purchases of commodities $1,\ldots,n-1$, (we use the traditional Hicksian weekly equilibrium concept), $x_n = m$ is holdings of nominal money balances at the end of the week, and P is the aggregate price level, subject to a budget constraint

(2) $$y + L = \sum_{i=1}^{n} p_i x_i$$

where y is income, L is the week's initial endowment of money balances, and p_i is the money price of commodity i, $i=1,\ldots,n-1$ (and where $p_n = 1$).

We assume, following Dusansky-Kalman and Patinkin, that

(3) $$P = P(p_1,\ldots,p_{n-1}).$$

And, for expository convenience, we make the usual assumption that $u(x_1,\ldots,x_n,P)$ has continuous second partials and $P(p_1,\ldots,p_{n-1})$ has continuous second partials.

Combining (1) and (3) we now consider the general problem of maximizing

(4) $$u = f(x_1,\ldots,x_{n-1},m,p_1,\ldots,p_{n-1})$$

with respect to $x_1,\ldots,x_{n-1}$ and m subject to (2), where for notational convenience we will write $x = (x_1,\ldots,x_{n-1})$, $p = (p_1,\ldots,p_{n-1})$[3]. The maximization of (4) with respect to (x,m) subject to (2) yields first order conditions which can be solved, under the usual conditions, for the demand functions:

$$(5) \qquad x_i = h^i(p,L,y), \quad i=1,\ldots,n-1,$$

$$(6) \qquad m = h^m(p,L,y).$$

These demand functions <u>do</u> exhibit money illusion.[4]

We now derive the most general conditions under which the commodity demand functions are homogeneous of degree zero in (p,L,y). By Euler's theorem on homogeneous functions we know

$$(7) \qquad h^i(p,L,y) = h^i(\alpha p, \alpha L, \alpha y) \text{ iff}$$

$$(8) \qquad \sum_{j=1}^{n-1} \frac{\partial h^i}{\partial p_j} p_j + \frac{\partial h^i}{\partial L} L + \frac{\partial h^i}{\partial y} y = 0, \quad i=1,\ldots,n-1.$$

---

[3] The objective function in (4) can be <u>formally derived</u> via a multi-period optimization model which posits that utility depends on consumption only, i.e. $u = u(x_t,x_{t+1})$, where x_t and x_{t+1} are the consumption vectors for periods x_t and x_{t+1}, respectively. See Grandmont (1974). Note also that we assume all prices positive and other variables nonnegative.

[4] For details see Dusansky and Kalman (1974), pp. 116-117.

However, from a total differentiation of the first order conditions we know that

$$\frac{\partial h^i}{\partial p_j} = \lambda \frac{D_{ji}}{D} - \sum_{k=1}^{n-1} \frac{\partial^2 f}{\partial x_k \partial p_j} \frac{D_{ki}}{D} - \frac{\partial^2 f}{\partial m \partial p_j} \frac{D_{ni}}{D} + x_j \frac{D_{n+1\, i}}{D},$$

$$\frac{\partial h^i}{\partial y} = \frac{\partial h^i}{\partial L} = - \frac{D_{n+1\, i}}{D} \quad [5]$$

where D is the determinant of the Jacobian of the first order conditions, D_{ji} is the cofactor of the element in row j column i of the Jacobian and λ is the Lagrange multiplier.

Hence, we have (8) iff

$$(9) \qquad \sum_{j=1}^{n-1} \left[\lambda \frac{D_{ji}}{D} - \sum_{k=1}^{n-1} \frac{\partial^2 f}{\partial x_k \partial p_j} \frac{D_{ki}}{D} - \frac{\partial^2 f}{\partial m \partial p_j} \frac{D_{ni}}{D} + x_j \frac{D_{n+1\, i}}{D} \right] p_j - [L+y] \frac{D_{n+1\, i}}{D} = 0.$$

Using (2) we have (9) iff

$$(10) \qquad \frac{\lambda}{D} \sum_{j=1}^{n-1} D_{ji} p_j - \sum_{j=1}^{n-1} \sum_{k=1}^{n-1} \frac{\partial^2 f}{\partial x_k \partial p_j} \frac{D_{ki}}{D} p_j - \sum_{j=1}^{n-1} \frac{\partial^2 f}{\partial m \partial p_j} \frac{D_{ni}}{D} p_j - m \frac{D_{n+1\, i}}{D} = 0.$$

However, by the theorem on expansion by alien cofactors, we know that $\sum_{j=1}^{n-1} D_{ji} P_j + D_{ni} = 0$, $i=1,\ldots,n-1$. Hence, since $D \neq 0$ by the second order conditions, (10) iff

$$(11) \qquad \sum_{j=1}^{n-1} \sum_{k=1}^{n-1} \frac{\partial^2 f}{\partial x_k \partial P_j} D_{ki} P_j + \sum_{j=1}^{n-1} \frac{\partial^2 f}{\partial m \partial P_j} D_{ni} P_j + \lambda D_{ni} + m D_{n+1 i} = 0.$$

---

[5] For a detailed derivation see Dusansky and Kalman (1972), pp. 343-5.

The condition in (11) constitutes the most general condition under which the commodity demand functions are homogeneous of degree zero, and thus completely characterizes the absence of money illusion outcome. It is true that (11) is a technical condition, not easily amenable to a direct economic interpretation. However, this is not highly unusual in economic theory. What is most important is that the technical results have useful economic implications. Some useful implications of (11) are:

(i) The iff condition contains the two sufficiency conditions thus far in the literature as special cases. As a result, both of these sufficiency conditions are now clearly seen to be overly restrictive.[6]

(ii) As a corollary to (i), we now know that the class of utility functions which yields the absence of money illusion result is larger than economists had previously believed it to be. This tells us that more diverse economic behavior (that is, a larger number of utility functions) is consistent with the illusion-free outcome.

(iii) Since (11) imposes no homogeneity assumption of any kind on either the utility function or on the marginal utility functions, we now know that one does not have to employ a homogeneity assumption to effect the homogeneity result.

(iv) Given the money illusion experiment, we now see that it is possible for the marginal rates of substitution to be affected by the price changes at the same time that observed

---

[6] Of course homogeneous utility functions and/or utility functions whose marginal utilities are homogeneous are admissible. However, they are not necessary.

demand remains unaltered. This implication contrasts sharply with each of the existing sufficiency conditions. Imposing homogeneity on the utility function or on the marginal utility functions implies that the marginal rate of substitution between any two commodities remains invariant when prices and initial holdings increase by some proportionality factor. This unrealistically restricts economic behavior. For example, in the case of two goods that are widely divergent in absolute prices (like bicycles and automobiles) the money illusion experiment, given a generalized real balance effect, may well have an impact on the marginal rate of substitution between them. Such an impact is precluded by the two sufficiency conditions. However, it is admissible (but not necessarily required) under the condition presented in (11). As a result, the underlying theory is extended to incorporate plausible economic behavior that previously lay outside the explanatory power of the model.

(v) As a corollary to (iv), since under the money illusion experiment the marginal rates of substitution are in general altered, we now know that there exist utility functions whose associated demand functions could <u>not</u> be equivalently derived from some "suitably" chosen homogeneous utility function. There is some set of illusion-free demand functions, no matter how small, which are consistent with the if and only if conditions and which <u>cannot</u> be derived from utility functions whose marginal rates of substitution are invariant (i.e., cannot be derived from utility functions that only satisfy one of the usual sufficiency conditions).

To <u>illustrate</u> the generality of the complete characterization in (11), we consider the simplest case, that of two commodities. Equation (11) now becomes:

$$(11') \qquad \sum_{j,k=1}^{2} \frac{\partial^2 f}{\partial x_k \partial p_j} \frac{D_{ki}}{D} p_j = p_1 p_2 \frac{\partial^2 f}{\partial x_1 \partial p_1} - p_1^2 \frac{\partial^2 f}{\partial x_2 \partial p_1} + p_2^2 \frac{\partial^2 f}{\partial x_1 \partial p_2} - p_1 p_2 \frac{\partial^2 f}{\partial x_2 \partial p_2} = 0.$$

This is a second order partial differential equation, a solution to which is the following utility function:

$$(12) \qquad u = f(p_1x_1+p_2x_2) + g\left(\frac{p_1}{p_2}, x_1, x_2\right).$$

This utility function is non-homogeneous. Its marginal utilities (which also depend on prices) are also non-homogeneous. However, it yields demand functions which are free of money illusion.[7] Note also that the marginal rate of substitution also depends on prices and thus need not be invariant under the money illusion experiment. Finally, the utility function in (12) is not separable in p and x. Prices and commodities can interact in a complex manner. This complexity obviously increases for $n > 2$.

---

[7] Verification is presented in the Appendix.

References

R.W. Clower and J.G. Riley, "The Foundations of Money Illusion in a Neoclassical Micro-Monetary Model: Comment," Amer. Econ. Rev., March 1976, Vol. 66, No. 1, 184-185.

R. Dusansky and P.J. Kalman, "The Real Balance Effect and the Traditional Theory of Consumer Behavior: A Reconciliation," J. Econ. Theory, Dec. 1972, 5, 336-47 and Erratum, 1973, 6, 107.

____________________, "The Foundation of Money Illusion in a Neoclassical Micro-Monetary Model," Amer. Econ. Rev., March 1974, LXIV, 1, 115-122.

____________________, "The Foundations of Money Illusion in a Neoclassical Micro-Monetary Model: Reply," Amer. Econ. Rev., March 1976, Vol. 66, No. 1, 192-195.

J.M. Grandmont, "On the Short-Run Equilibrium in a Monetary Economy," in J. Dreze, ed., Allocation Under Uncertainty, Macmillan, New York, 1974, pp. 213-228.

J. Marschak, "Money Illusion and Demand Analysis," Review of Economics and Statistics, February, 1943.

D. Patinkin, Money, Interest, and Prices, 2nd ed., New York, 1965.

P.A. Samuelson, The Foundations of Economic Analysis, Cambridge, 1947.

Appendix

We now show that

$$(12) \qquad u = f(p_1x_1+p_2x_2) + g(\frac{p_1}{p_2}, x_1, x_2)$$

satifies the complete characterization in (11'). Appropriate differentiation of (12) yields: (let $\alpha = p_1x_1 + p_2x_2$ and $\beta = \frac{p_1}{p_2}$)

$$\frac{\partial^2 f}{\partial x_2 \partial p_1} = x_1 \frac{\partial^2 f}{\partial^2 \alpha} p_2 + \frac{1}{p_2} \frac{\partial^2 g}{\partial \beta \partial x_2}$$

$$\frac{\partial^2 f}{\partial x_1 \partial p_1} = \frac{\partial f}{\partial \alpha} + x_1 \frac{\partial^2 f}{\partial^2 \alpha} p_1 + \frac{1}{p_2} \frac{\partial^2 g}{\partial \beta \partial x_1}$$

$$\frac{\partial^2 f}{\partial x_2 \partial p_2} = \frac{\partial f}{\partial \alpha} + x_2 \frac{\partial^2 f}{\partial^2 \alpha} p_2 - \frac{p_1}{p_2^2} \frac{\partial^2 g}{\partial \beta \partial x_2}$$

$$\frac{\partial^2 f}{\partial x_1 \partial p_2} = x_2 \frac{\partial^2 f}{\partial^2 \alpha} p_1 - \frac{p_1}{p_2^2} \frac{\partial^2 g}{\partial \beta \partial x_1} .$$

Direct substitution into (11') shows that it is satisfied.

Abstract

Chichilnisky, Graciela
Kalman, Peter J.

Comparative Statics of Less Neoclassical Agents

The study of the optimization problems of demand and producer theories is extended to models where agents exhibit more complex characteristics than those of the neoclassical agent. Here the objective functions are parameterized, there may be many, not necessarily linear constraints, and non convexities in both the objectives and the constraints. We study generic differentiability properties of the optimal solutions. We also give a generalized Slutsky type decomposition, and sufficient conditions on the objective and constraints for its symmetry and negative semidefiniteness.

Comparative Statics of Less Neoclassical Agents

G. Chichilnisky [1]
Economics Department
Harvard University

P. J. Kalman [1]
Harvard University and SUNY at Stony Brook

August 1976
(revised March 1977)

Introduction

In recent years demand and producer theories have been extended to models where the economic agents exhibit more complex characteristics than those of the neoclassical agent. [2] The optimization problem of these less neoclassical agents includes cases where the objective functions depend also on parameters, there are many (not necessarily linear) constraints, and non-convexities. For example, agents' preferences among commodity bundles may be parametrized or influenced by prices as in Veblen and Scitovsky models [6], [3], or real balances may enter the utility functions [9]. Other models where the objective functions are parameterized are those of choice under uncertainty and with imperfect information. Nonconvexities on the

---

[1] This research was supported by NSF Grant GS 18174. P. J. Kalman is visiting Harvard from SUNY at Stony Brook. The authors thank K. J. Arrow, T. Muench and T. Rader for insightful suggestions and a referee for helpful comments.

[2] For example, in neoclassical consumer theory the objective function (utility) is usually assumed to be concave, the constraint (budget) linear, and no parameters affect the utilities. In producer models, there is usually only one constraint, and convexity assumptions are in general made.

side of the constraints (technology) are naturally induced by informational variables; in models with uncertainty as many constraints may appear as states of nature.

A natural question concerning the models discussed above is to what extent do the comparative statics results of the neoclassical theory still apply. In particular, since it is known that the Slutsky matrix and its properties of symmetry and negative semi-definiteness are not preserved in general [6], one can, at most, hope to obtain conditions on the classes of models (classes of objective functions and constraint functions) in which these properties are still satisfied. [3]

Even though by nature comparative static properties are essentially local, the techniques involved so far in their proofs mostly used arguments requiring convexity assumptions of the objective and constraint functions. Since comparative static theorems concern the signs of partial derivatives in some neighborhood of an equilibrium point, these global assumptions place more stringent restrictions on the objective and constraint functions than seem necessary. [4]

Theorems 1 and 2 contain local results about solutions to a general class of constrained maximization models; in Theorem 1 we study generic differentiability of the solutions and in Theorem 2 we

[3]These properties have been recovered for certain separable classes of objective and constraint functions in some of these more general types of models, mostly under convexity assumptions and with special restrictions for each particular case. [7].

[4]Since 1970 there has been an upsurge in the study of local properties of equilibria starting with the leading article by G. Debreu who introduced tools of differential topology to study, among others, problems of existence, local uniqueness and stability of equilibria [5]. Independently, interest in local properties arose from models where there may be many equilibria positions, for instance, when the utilities cost or production functions are not necessarily convex (concave).

give a generalized Slutsky type decomposition. The techniques used in Theorem 1 to obtain generic differentiability of the solutions are related to those of Debreu [5], who parametrizes the agents by their endowments in a general equilibrium model, and Smale [12]. However, even though the parameters of the objectives and contraints include elements of (both finite and infinite dimensional) function spaces, here we do not use Thom's transversality theorem as in [12]. The genericity in these parameters is proven directly by use of Sard's theorem [1] and further technical arguments, and with respect to a topology described by the proximity of the values of the functions and their derivatives, which seems to be natural for spaces of economic agents. However, this restricts the results to compact subspaces of the commodity space. These results admit an extension to noncompact commodity spaces if one uses the Whitney topology as, for example, in [12] or [8]. The derivation of the generalized Slutsky operator of Theorem 2 becomes more complicated here than in the usual models because of the many constraints, and the operator obtained is of a slightly different nature. One reason is that compensation can be performed in different manners here, since there are many constraints. Also, the existence of parameters induces new effects that do not exist in nonparametrized models, and the classical properties of symmetry and negative semi-definiteness are not, in general, preserved [6]. Finally, we consider in this paper, for the case of models with price dependent preferences, those preferences where the objects of choice are "quantity-price situations" also called unconditional preferences. An alternative way of looking at price dependent preferences, which this paper does not consider, is where the objects of choice are only quantities, for a fixed set of prices, also called conditional preferences; for a discussion, see, for instance, [3] and [10]. The "compensated" demand functions are only defined in the case of unconditional preferences [10]. Our results apply to cases of households and firms with unconditional preferences. Propositions 1 and 2 give sufficient conditions for recovering symmetry and negative semi-definiteness properties in our general framework. Results related to this paper are contained in [4].

We first prove some generic results on local uniqueness, differentiability and Slutsky type decompositions of optimal solutions to constrained optimization problems with parameters entering the objective function and constraints--which can be linear or nonlinear. This formulation contains the models discussed above, and also the neoclassical producer and consumer models. Convexity assumptions on either the objective functions or the constraints are not required; the special cases where the objective function is concave and increasing and the constraints are convex yield optimal functions--as opposed to correspondences--with the above properties.

The problem studied here is that of an agent maximizing a constrained objective:

$$(P) \qquad \max_{x \in X} f(x, a) \qquad \text{subject to} \quad g(x, a) = b$$

where X is a compact subset of R^{n+} whose interior[5] is diffeomorphic to a ball in R^n, $a \in A$, $b \in B$, A and B are similar type subsets of R^{m+} and $R^{\ell+}$, respectively, and $n > \ell$. An agent is characterized by an objective function f and by a constraint g. Therefore, the space of all possible agents can be identified with the product of the space of admissible objectives and constraints. Let the space of objective functions denoted D be $C^k(X \times A, R^+)$, the space of maps from $X \times A$ to R^+ which are increasing in x and k-times continuously differentiable in a neighborhood of $X \times A$, and let the space of constraints denoted E be $C^k(X \times A, B)$, where $k \geq 2$.

[5] R^{n+} denotes the positive orthant of R^n.

We now briefly discuss the topology of the function spaces we consider. Let Y be a compact ball. Then the space $C^k(Y, R)$ can be given the C^k norm topology defined by:

$$\|f\|_k = \sup_{y \in Y} \{|f(y)|, |D^1 f(y)|, \dots, |D^k f(y)|\}$$

where $D^i f$ denotes the i-th derivative of f. Let $\overline{D}$ denote a C^1 bounded subset of D.[6] We shall also consider here the special cases of increasing concave objective functions and convex constraints: Let D_0 be the space of C^k functions f defined on a neighborhood of $X \times A$ with values in R^+ which are increasing and concave on the variable $x \in X$, and let $E_0 \subset E$ be the subset of functions of $C^k(X \times A, B)$ which are convex on $x \in X$. Let $\overline{D}_0$ denote $\overline{D} \cap D_0$.

In the next result we study properties of the optimal solutions to problem (P), denoted $h_{f,g}(a,b)$. Note that $h_{f,g}(a,b)$ is, in general, a correspondence.[7] A solution is called interior if it is contained in the interior of the set X.

---

6 This assumption on $\overline{D}$, which does not imply compactness of $\overline{D}$, could be weakened by the use of different topologies on D, such as those of [12], [8].

7 In the classical consumer case $h_{f,g}(a,b)$ represents the demand vector, x a commodity bundle, $b \in R^+$ income, and a the price vector. Also, $g(x,a) = x \cdot a = b$ represents the budget constraint and $f(x,a) = u(x)$ the utility function.

THEOREM 1. <u>For an open and dense set of objective functions</u> f <u>in</u> $\overline{D}$, <u>and any given constraint</u> g <u>in</u> E, <u>the interior solutions of problem</u> (P) <u>above define locally unique</u> C^1 <u>functions</u> $h_{f,g}(a,b)$ <u>on a subset of</u> $A \times B$ <u>which contains an open and dense set.</u> <u>This is also true for the globally defined</u> $h_{f,g}(a,b)$ <u>for</u> f <u>in</u> $\overline{D}_0$ <u>and</u> g <u>in</u> E_0.

<u>Proof:</u> For any g in E, let

$$\psi: \overline{D} \times A \times B \to C^{k-1}(X \times R^{\ell}, R^n \times B)$$

be defined by

$$\psi(f,a,b)(x,\lambda) = \left(\frac{\partial}{\partial x} f + \lambda \frac{\partial}{\partial x} g,\ g-b\right)$$

where $\lambda \in R^{\ell}$.

We first note that for each a, b in $A \times B$, $\psi(\cdot, a, b)$ is continuous as a function on $\overline{D}$ since the map

$$\partial: C^k(X,R) \to C^{k-1}(X,R^n)$$

defined by

$$f \to \frac{\partial}{\partial x} f$$

is continuous in the respective C^k and C^{k-1} topologies. Thus, ψ is itself a continuous map.

We now consider the restriction of $\psi(f,a,b)$ on $X \times B_0$, where B_0 is a compact ball of R^{ℓ} which contains the λ's in the kernel of

$\psi(f,a,b)(x,\cdot)$ for $x \in X$.[8] For simplicity, denote $\psi(f,a,b)|_{X \times B_0}$ by $\psi(f,a,b)$.

Let $B_1 = X \times B_0$. Thus,

$$\psi(f,a,b) \in C^{k-1}(B_1, R^n \times B) \quad .$$

Let θ be the set of maps ξ in $C^{k-1}(B_1, R^n \times B)$ such that $\xi \pitchfork 0$.[9] Since B_1 is compact, by the openness of transversality theorem (see [1]), θ is an open set.

Consider now the restriction of the C^{k-1} norm topology on the subset I of $C^{k-1}(B_1, R^n \times B)$, where I is the image of $\overline{D} \times A \times B$ under ψ. Let $\overline{\theta} = \theta \cap I$ and let I inherit the relative topology, and let $\overline{\psi}$ be defined as equal to ψ on the domain of ψ, but having I as its image. Then $\overline{\theta} = \theta \cap I$ is open in the relative topology of I and by continuity of $\overline{\psi}$, $\overline{\psi}^{-1}(\overline{\theta})$ is also open in $\overline{D} \times A \times B$. Note that $\overline{\psi}^{-1}(\theta)$ is contained in the set of elements in $\overline{D} \times A \times B$ such that the corresponding interior optimal solutions $h_{f,g}(a,b)$ of (P) define locally a

---

8 We define $\psi(f,a,b)$ on a subset of $X \times R^{\ell}$ which includes all x in X and those λ's given by the zeros of the first order conditions of $\psi(f,a,b)(x,\cdot)$ for some $x \in X$. By [11, p. 30], for all $x \in X$ and for all (f,a,b) in $\overline{D} \times A \times B$ the respective $\overline{\lambda}$'s in the kernel of $\psi(f,a,b)(x,\cdot)$ are contained in some compact ball B_0 of R^{ℓ}.

9 Let M and N be C^k manifolds, $f: M \to N$ a C^k map. We say that f is transversal to a point $y \in N$ denoted by $f \pitchfork y$ if whenever $y = f(x)$, i.e., $x \in f^{-1}(y)$, then $Df(x)$ is onto, where $Df(x)$ represents the derivative of the map f computed at x, a linear map from the tangent space of M at x to the tangent space of N at y. A point x in M is a critical point if and only if $Df(x)$ is not onto; x is a regular point if it is not a critical point. y is a critical value if there exists a critical point x in M with $y = f(x)$; y is a regular value if and only if it is not a critical value (see [1]).

unique C^1 function[10] by the implicit function theorem (since $\frac{\partial}{\partial x, \lambda} \psi(f,a,b)$ is regular at the kernel of $\psi(f,a,b)$ if and only if it is invertible). Hence, for an open set of objective functions in $\overline{D}$, and an open set of parameters in $A \times B$, the interior solutions of (P) define locally unique functions which are C^1.

By Sard's theorem, (see [1]) since $k \geq 1$, the set of regular values of $\overline{\psi}(f,a,b)$ is dense in $R^n \times B$. Then, for any $\epsilon > 0$, let $(q,k) \in R^n \times B$ be a regular value of the map $\overline{\psi}(f,a,b)$ with $\|q,k\| < \epsilon$. Define $\overline{\psi}^{\epsilon}$ by:

$$\overline{\psi}^{\epsilon}(f,a,b) = \psi(f,a,b) - (q,k) .$$

Note that $\overline{\psi}^{\epsilon}(f,a,b) \pitchfork 0$ iff (q,k) is a regular value of $\overline{\psi}(f,a,b)$. If $\overline{f} = f - qx$, and $\overline{b} = b - k$, then $\overline{\psi}^{\epsilon}(f,a,b) = \overline{\psi}(\overline{f},a,\overline{b})$. Since X is compact, $\overline{f}$ can be taken to be arbitrarily close to f in the C^k norm by choosing ϵ small enough, and similarly, $\overline{b}$ can be chosen arbitrarily close to b. Therefore, since 0 is a regular value of $\overline{\psi}^{\epsilon}(f,a,b)$, then $(\overline{f},a,\overline{b}) \in \overline{\psi}^{-1}(\overline{\theta})$, and thus $\overline{\psi}^{-1}(\overline{\theta})$ is also dense in $\overline{D} \times A \times B$.

If f is concave and g convex, i.e., if f is in $\overline{D}_0$ and g in $\overline{E}_0 = E_0 \cap \overline{E}$, then the above results also apply, proving in this case that the globally defined optimal functions of the agents are C^1 on an open and dense subset of $A \times B$ and of objective functions and constraints f and g in $\overline{D}_0 \times \overline{E}_0$. This completes the proof.

---

10 There might be elements in $\overline{D} \times A \times B$ such that the corresponding $h_{f,g}(a,b)$ defines a C^1 function, but are not contained in $\overline{\psi}^{-1}(\theta)$ since $(\partial/\partial x, \lambda)\psi(f,a,b)$ may be singular. Also, the boundary solutions to (P) may not be contained in $\overline{\psi}^{-1}(\theta)$.

Remarks.

1. Note that the results of Theorem 1 are restricted to interior solutions of problem (P); solutions to (P) always exist by compactness of X. If the objective function f is required to have all its hypersurfaces (or indifference surfaces) contained in the interior of X, then it would follow that all solutions to (P) are interior. However, since X is compact, this would imply some satiation of the maximizing agent. When the choice space is R^{n+} a standard assumption is to require that the indifference surfaces be contained in the interior of R^{n+}, in which case all solutions are interior. This boundary condition does not imply satiation since R^{n+} is not compact.[11]

2. Let $\overline{E}$ be a C^1 bounded subset of E. Then if the map ψ of Theorem 1 is defined instead as:

$$\psi: \overline{D} \times \overline{E} \times A \times B \rightarrow C^{k-1}(X \times R^{\ell}, R^n \times B)$$

by

$$\psi(f, a, b)(x, \lambda) = \left(\frac{\partial}{\partial x} f + \lambda \frac{\partial}{\partial x} g,\ g-b\right)$$

a similar proof would yield open density of the set of objective functions and constraints in which the results of Theorem 1 are true, instead of a fixed constraint g.

We next prove existence of a Slutsky-type decomposition for the interior solutions to problem (P) above. Note that such a decomposition can only be defined in a neighborhood of (a, b) if h(a, b) is a C^1 function at (a, b).

---

[11] The results of Theorem 1 can be extended to the case where X is R^{n+} by the use of different topologies on spaces of C^k functions, such as the Whitney topology [12], [8].

Assume $k > \ell$. For a given f and g a necessary condition for x to be an interior maximum is the existence of a λ in R^{ℓ} such that

$$\frac{\partial}{\partial x} f(x,a) + \lambda \frac{\partial}{\partial x} g(x,a) = 0 \quad ,$$

(1) and

$$g(x,a) = b \quad .$$

For a proof of the next theorem, see [4].

THEOREM 2. Let $g \in E$ be regular.[12] For an open and dense set of objective functions f and parameters a in $\overline{D} \times A$, if the corresponding Lagrangian multiplier λ of (1) is strictly positive, and Z defined below exists,[13] then there exists locally a Slutsky-type decomposition S(a, b) into linear operators, given by:[14]

$$(2) \qquad S(a,b) \equiv \frac{\partial}{\partial a} h + \frac{\partial}{\partial b} h\left(\frac{\partial}{\partial a} g\right)$$

$$= \frac{\partial}{\partial a} h\Big|_{f=f_0} + \frac{\partial}{\partial b} h\left(\phi\left(\frac{\partial}{\partial a} g\right) - \mu\left(\frac{\partial}{\partial a} f\right)\right)$$

$$= -\left[\left(\frac{\partial^2}{\partial x^2} L\right)^{-1} + \left(\frac{\partial^2}{\partial x^2} L\right)^{-1}\left(\frac{\partial}{\partial x} g\right) Z \left(\frac{\partial}{\partial x} g\right)\left(\frac{\partial^2}{\partial x^2} L\right)^{-1}\right]\left(\frac{\partial^2}{\partial x \partial a} L\right)$$

where $L(x, a, \lambda, b)$ denotes $f(x,a) + \lambda(g(x,a) - b)$,

---

[12] i. e., $\frac{\partial}{\partial x} g(x,a)$ is onto for all x and a.

[13] Existence and density of such λ's is discussed in [2]. Generic existence of Z can be proven following the techniques of Theorem 1 also.

[14] Transposes of matrices are not indicated.

$$Z = -\left[\left(\frac{\partial}{\partial x} g\right)\left(\frac{\partial^2}{\partial x^2} L\right)^{-1}\left(\frac{\partial}{\partial x} g\right)\right]^{-1},$$

and ϕ and μ are defined as follows:

$$\mu = \left(0, \ldots, 0, \overset{\text{i-th place}}{\frac{1}{\lambda_i}}, 0, \ldots, 0\right)$$

and

$$\phi = (\phi_{q,r}), \qquad q = 1, \ldots, \ell, \qquad r = 1, \ldots, \ell,$$

$$\phi_{q,r} = 1 \qquad \text{if } q = r, \; q \neq i$$

$$0 \qquad \text{if } q \neq r \text{ and } q \neq i$$

$$\phi_{i,r} = -\frac{\lambda_r}{\lambda_i} \qquad \text{if } r \neq i$$

$$\phi_{i,i} = 0 ;$$

if $b \in R^1$, $\phi = 0$.

<u>If</u> $f \in \overline{D}_0$ <u>and</u> $g \in \overline{E}_0$ <u>the above results hold globally</u>.

Note that the term

$$\frac{\partial}{\partial b} h \left(\phi \frac{\partial}{\partial a} g - \mu \frac{\partial}{\partial a} f \right)$$

of the decomposition of S(a, b) depends on the choice of the index i through the operators μ and ϕ. Thus the middle term of the equation (2) depends on the choice of the particular constraint which is used for the compensation (denoted by the index i in the definition of the operators). However, S(a, b) as given by the first and third expressions, does not depend on the choice of the index. In the cases of optimization models with only one constraint, the compensation can be done in only one way; in general, one can choose as many ways of "compensation" as there are constraints, and more: any linear combination of the constraints, for instance, could also be used as a compensating parameter, and a similar proof will follow. The basic point here is that when df = 0 (on the surface f = constant), the components of the differential form db are not all linearly independent. Different choices or representations of this linear dependence (of which a particular case is that given by the operators ϕ and μ) would yield different forms of the terms of the middle expression of (2). When considering this particular expression in the middle of Equation (2), which can be thought of as a "modified substitution effect", these degrees of freedom in the choice of the compensating parameter may allow one to adopt a particular way of compensation depending on the type of economic model under consideration and depending on the properties one wants to study in each particular model.

In this general framework the classical properties of symmetry and negative semi-definiteness are not, in general, preserved [6]. In Propositions 1 and 2 below, we exhibit some forms of objective functions and constraint functions for which $S(a, b)$ has these properties under certain conditions. For proofs of the next two propositions, see [4].

PROPOSITION 1. Assume the objective function $f(x, a)$ has the form

(i) $$f \equiv \gamma[a \cdot x] + f^1(x) + f^2(a)$$

and the constraints $g(x, a)$ have the form

(ii) $$g^i \equiv \delta^i[a \cdot x] + g^{i1}(x) + g^{i2}(a) , \qquad i = 1, 2, \ldots, \ell$$

and that all the conditions for existence of the matrix $S(a, b)$ of Section 1 are satisfied, γ, $\delta^i \in R_+$. Then $S(a, b)$ is symmetric when $m = n$ in problem (P).

PROPOSITION 2. Under the conditions of Proposition 1, if $f \in D_0$ and $g \in E_0$, the matrix $S(a, b)$ is negative semi-definite when $\gamma + \Sigma_i \lambda_i \delta^i \geq 0$, and where $\lambda = (\lambda_1, \ldots, \lambda_\ell)$ is the corresponding "Lagrangian multiplier".

References

1. Abraham, R. and J. Robbin, Transversal Mappings and Flows, (W.A. Benjamin, Inc., New York, 1967).

2. Arrow, K. J., E. Barankin, and D. Blackwell, "Admissible Points of Convex Sets", Contributions to the Theory of Games, (Princeton, 1953), 87-92.

3. Arrow, K. J. and F.H. Hahn, General Competitive Analysis, (Holden-Day, San Francisco, 1971).

4. Chichilnisky, G. and P. J. Kalman, "Properties of Critical Points and Operators in Economics", Journal of Mathematical Analysis and Applications, February 1977, 340-349.

5. Debreu, G., "Economies with a Finite Set of Equilibria", Econometrica, 38, 1970, 387-392.

6. Kalman, P. J., "Theory of Consumer Behavior when Prices Enter the Utility Function", Econometrica, Vol. 36, No. 3-4, October, 1968, 497-510.

7. Kalman, P. J. and M. Intriligator, "Generalized Comparative Statics with Applications to Consumer Theory and Producer Theory", International Economic Review, Vol. 14, No. 2, June 1973, 473-486.

8. Kalman, P. J. and K. P. Lin, "Applications of Thom's Transversality Theory and Brouwer Degree Theory to Economics", Journal of Mathematical Analysis and Applications, forthcoming.

9. Patinkin, D., Money, Interest, and Prices, 2nd edition (New York: Harper and Row, 1965).

10. Pollak, R.A., "Price Dependent Preferences", American Economic Review. forthcoming.

11. Rad er, T., Theory of Microeconomics, (Academic Press, New York, 1972).

12. Smale, S., "Global Analysis and Economics, IIA", Journal of Mathematical Economics, 1, 1974, 1-14.

On Some Properties of Short-Run Monetary Equilibrium with Uncertain Expectations*

by

Peter J. Kalman and Kuan-Pin Lin

August 1977

I. Introduction

We shall consider a short-run or temporary equilibrium framework, which can be viewed as a general Walrasian equilibrium analysis of a sequence of markets over time, where at each date each agent makes decisions according to his expectations of the future. The expectations are formed in the light of the agents' knowledge of the past history of the economy. In this framework it is very natural to introduce a financial asset such as money and study the equilibrium properties of a money economy. These ideas go back to Hicks [14] and were adopted by Patinkin [21] in his integration of monetary and value theories. More recent contributions to short-run equilibrium theory can be found in the works of Arrow and Hahn [2] and Stigum [26]. Recent contributions to short-run monetary equilibrium theory can be found in the works of Grandmont [13], Hool [16], Sondermann [25] and Younès [28], among others. In these works, the expectations of future events taken as data of the system play an important role in determining the existence of a

---

*We thank K. J. Arrow, M. W. Hirsch, G. Laroque, A. Phillips, and J. Wolf for helpful comments and suggestions.

monetary equilibrium. Also at equilibrium, the price of money is positive although money has no intrinsic value for the current consumption.

As pointed out by Debreu in [6] and [7], once there is a general solution to the existence problem, one should investigate the structure of the set of equilibria. Otherwise, the explanation of equilibrium is totally indeterminate. First, there may exist infinitely many equilibria. Also, the economic system may be unstable in the sense that a small change of economic data would lead to an entirely different set of equilibria. Therefore, it is highly desirable to have an economy for which the set of equilibria is locally unique (i. e., discrete) and stable (i. e., continuous). These properties are also needed if one wants to study the comparative statics of the system.

Using techniques of differential topology recently introduced into the economics literature by Debreu [6], [7] and Smale [23], [24], we establish, for the first time, the properties of local uniqueness and stability of short-run monetary equilibria under uncertainty for "almost all" money economies as well as existence for every money economy. As pointed out by Hicks, "people rarely have <u>precise</u> expectations at all, . . . but partake more of the character of probability distributions" (see [14], p. 125 and p. 133). For the present study the formation of particular forms of expectations is not essential. The crucial assumptions are sufficient differentiability of the direct utility functions and expectation functions. [1] Differentiability of expectations is also considered

---

[1] The differentiability assumptions are not unreasonable since the approximation theorems ensure that any continuous function can be approximated by a differentiable function.

by Fuchs and Laroque [12] and Fuchs [11] for a different model. Their analysis emphasizes the (long-run) dynamic behavior of a sequence of equilibria using a demand function approach with point expectations, that is, no uncertainty in the model. In particular, they prove, under certain conditions, that the equilibria are locally unique and stable and also that the asymptotic stability of (stationary) equilibria is preserved under small perturbations in the point expectations of the agents. Our paper concerns itself mainly with the questions of comparative statics of a temporary general equilibrium process in which the agents' expectations of the future environment take the form of probability measures. Moreover, we study utility functions directly and do not require well defined demand functions as in [12] and [11]. Our class of utility functions includes those which define continuously differentiable demand functions.

In Section II some basic definitions and assumptions are made and discussed. Among them, a set of classical assumptions are postulated on the future market which guarantee the differentiability requirement in the model. Also, as usual, a compactness assumption on the expectations is made for the analysis (see for instance [13], [16], [25] and [28]). Section III formulates an (infinite dimensional) space of money economies in which an element is a list of expectation functions (not point expectations as in [12] and [11]), directly utility functions, money and commodity endowments. These are all variables in our model. That is, we allow beliefs, preferences and initial holdings to vary in a general way. A useful technical concept of "extended" monetary equilibrium is introduced, which contains (classical) monetary equilibrium for every money economy. In Section IV the topological concept of ''almost all'' economies is introduced in the space of money economies. Two theorems, local uniqueness and stability, are presented and proved for ''almost all'' money economies using transversality theory of differential topology. The former can be obtained without assuming concavity of the utility functions for any agents. Finally, in Section V, the existence of short-run monetary equilibrium is proved by demonstrating that every money economy is a continuous deformation of an economy with unique equilibrium. The technique we use in this section is degree theory of differential topology.

II. The Model

We consider a framework of short-run monetary equilibrium theory with two successive periods where fiat money is used as the only store of value but gives no direct utility to the agents. Taking into consideration future (market and individual) uncertainty, the function of fiat money as a link of transferring wealth between periods provides some motives for holding money itself. In this section the basic definitions of the model are given. The analysis is an "interior analysis" which considers only positive price systems and each agent owns at least a little of each commodity (except money).

II(a) Basic Definitions

Suppose there are two periods t and $t+1$. For each period, there are ℓ commodities and n agents.[2] Let $P = \{x \in R^{\ell}: x \gg 0\}$[3] be the commodity space in which an element x^{ht} is a final consumption for agent h, $(h = 1, \ldots, n)$, at time t. We assume as usual that all ℓ commodities are perishable and have to be consumed during one period. Let $R_+ = \{x \in R: x \geq 0\}$ and $m^{ht} \in R_+$ is the h-th agent's money holding at time t. We note that money can be stored at no cost and held between periods t and $t+1$. However, it provides no direct satisfaction from consumption to the agents, and hence the holding of money could be zero for some agents. Let $S = \{(s^t, 1) \in R^{\ell+1}: s^t \gg 0\}$

---

[2] This can be generalized in a straightforward way to a different number of commodities and agents in periods t and $t+1$, respectively and to many periods.

[3] If $x, x' \in R^{\ell}$, $x \geq x'$ means $x_i \geq x_i'$ for all i; $x > x'$ means $x \geq x'$ and $x \neq x'$; $x \gg x'$ means $x_i > x_i'$ for all i.

be the monetary price space, where the price of money is given as unity and s^t is the price system of ℓ commodities at time t in terms of money. As agents are only interested in relative prices between money and commodities, we write

$$\Pi = \left\{ \pi^t = (p^t, p_0^t) \in R^{\ell+1}: \; p_0^t = \frac{1}{\sum_{i=1}^{\ell} s_i^t + 1} \text{ and } p_i^t = \frac{s_i^t}{\sum_{i=1}^{\ell} s_i^t + 1}, \; i = 1, \ldots, \ell, \text{ a d } (s^t, 1) \in S \right\}$$

to be the price space.

At the beginning of period t, every agent h in an economy knows with certainty his initial commodity and money endowments, i.e., $(\bar{x}^{ht}, m^{ht-1}) \in P \times R_+$, where the money endowment m^{ht-1} is the cash balance carried over from the previous period and we assume $\Sigma_{h=1}^{n} m^{ht-1} > 0$. The h-th agent's action is defined by a pair of commodity and money holdings, or $(x^{ht}, m^{ht}) \in P \times R_+$. A consequence of an action is a pair of current and future commodity consumptions denoted by $(x^{ht}, x^{ht+1}) \in P \times P$. Moreover, given $\bar{x}^{ht}$ and m^{ht-1}, the wealth of agent h at time t is defined by $y^{ht} = p^t \cdot \bar{x}^{ht} + p_0^t \cdot m^{ht-1}$ for each $\pi^t = (p^t, p_0^t) \in \Pi$. The budget set of agent h at period t is

$$B^{ht}(\pi^t, y^{ht}) = \{(x^{ht}, m^{ht}) \in P \times R_+: \; p^t \cdot x^{ht} + p_0^t \cdot m^{ht} = y^{ht}\} .$$

II(b) Expectation Functions

For each agent h, the strategy of choosing a consequence of an action at time t involves a plan $\hat{x}^{ht+1}$ made for the future consumption. Intuitively, a plan of an agent must be influenced by his view of the future environment. To specify a subjective uncertainty about the future environment for each agent, one assumes that the agent forecasts future prices and commodity endowments which take the form of probability distributions on $\Pi \times P$. In general, this forecast will depend on the current and past information available in the model. For a simple case, such an anticipation is assumed to rely upon the currently quoted price system π^t. More precisely, for each $\pi^t \in \Pi$ the agent's expectations can be described by a mapping $\gamma^h: \Pi \to \mathcal{M}(\Pi \times P)$ where $\mathcal{M}(\Pi \times P)$ is the set of probability measures defined on the measure space $(\Pi \times P, \mathcal{B}(\Pi \times P))$ with $\mathcal{B}(\Pi \times P)$ denoting the Borel σ-field of $\Pi \times P$. Then, for every $A \in \mathcal{B}(\Pi \times P)$, $\gamma^h(\pi^t; A)$ is the probability of A if π^t is quoted on the t-th market. For each $\pi^t \in \Pi$, the support of a probability measure $\gamma^h(\pi^t)$ denoted $\operatorname{supp} \gamma^h(\pi^t)$ is well defined (see [20]). It is the smallest closed set in $\Pi \times P$ with full measure. It is natural to impose a topology of weak convergence of probability measures on $\mathcal{M}(\Pi \times P)$ (see [20] for a definition and also [3]) and we make the following assumption:

<u>A. 1.</u> For each agent h, γ^h is continuously differentiable, i.e., $\gamma^h \in C^1(\Pi, \mathcal{M}(\Pi \times P))$, and $\operatorname{supp} \gamma^h(\pi^t)$ is compact for each $\pi^t \in \Pi$.

Since $\Pi \times P$ is a separable metric space, so is $\mathcal{M}(\Pi \times P)$ (see [20], Chap. II, Theorem 6.2). We shall use a metric on $\mathcal{M}(\Pi \times P)$, which has the advantage of being defined by a norm on a linear space, so that $\mathcal{M}(\Pi \times P)$ can be given a differentiable structure of a Banach space and the metric topology coincides with the topology of weak convergence on $\mathcal{M}(\Pi \times P)$ (see [8] for the construction of this metric). That is, the space of continuous differentiable functions from Π to $\mathcal{M}(\Pi \times P)$, denoted

$C^1(\Pi, \mathcal{M}(\Pi \times P))$, is well defined. The assumption that γ^h is class C^1 has also been used in [12] and [11] for a different model in a special sense: point expectations, i.e., no uncertainty. The idea of assuming compact support of expectations is in [13] and [28], among others. It is standard in the temporary equilibrium analysis. Let Γ be <u>the space of</u> expectations satisfying A. 1 for each agent h. In other words,

$$\Gamma = \{\gamma^h \in C^1(\Pi, \mathcal{M}(\Pi \times P)) : \text{supp}\, \gamma^h(\pi^t) \text{ is compact for each } \pi^t \in \Pi\}$$

For an action (x^{ht}, m^{ht}) and a price system π^t, analogous to the definitions of y^{ht} and $B^{ht}(\pi^t, y^{ht})$, the wealth of agent h at time t+1 is defined by $y^{ht+1} = p^{t+1} \cdot \bar{x}^{ht+1} + p_0^{t+1} \cdot m^{ht}$ for a future event $(\pi^{t+1}, \bar{x}^{ht+1})$. For convention we let $m^{ht+1} = 0$ and hence

$$B^{ht+1}(\pi^{t+1}, y^{ht+1}) = \{x^{ht+1} \in P : p^{t+1} \cdot x^{ht+1} = y^{ht+1}\}$$

for each $(\pi^{t+1}, \bar{x}^{ht+1}) \in \Pi \times P$.

II(c) von Neumann-Morgenstern Utility Functions

For each h, the agent's intertemporal preferences among consequences (satisfying Expected Utility Hypothesis) can be represented by a von Neumann-Morgenstern utility function u^h which is a bounded and continuous real-valued function from the consequence space $P \times P$ to the real line R. In order to use tools of differential topology we need the utility function to be sufficiently differentiable. We assume $u^h \in C^k(P \times P, R)$, $k > 2$, for each agent h and u^h is bounded. We further assume that u^h has the property that indifference surfaces do not intersect the boundary of the consequence space (see [7]), and that u^h satisfies a monotonicity hypothesis. Formally, we have the following:

A. 2. (i) $\overline{u^{h^{-1}}(c)} \subset P \times P$ for each $c \in R$, and

(ii) $D u^h(x^{ht}, x^{ht+1}) \gg 0$ for every $(x^{ht}, x^{ht+1}) \in P \times P$

where $\overline{u^{h^{-1}}(c)}$ is the closure of indifference surface $u^{h^{-1}}(c)$ and $Du^h(x^{ht}, x^{ht+1}) = (D_{x^{ht}} u^h(x^{ht}, x^{ht+1}), D_{x^{ht+1}} u^h(x^{ht}, x^{ht+1}))$ with

$$D_{x^{ht}} u^h(x^{ht}, x^{ht+1}) = \left(\partial u^h(x^{ht}, x^{ht+1})/\partial x_1^{ht}, \ldots, \partial u^h(x^{ht}, x^{ht+1})/\partial x_\ell^{ht}\right)$$

and

$$D_{x^{ht+1}} u^h(x^{ht}, x^{ht+1}) = (\partial u^h(x^{ht}, x^{ht+1})/\partial x_1^{ht+1}, \ldots, \partial u^h(x^{ht}, x^{ht+1})/\partial x_\ell^{ht+1}).$$

If one lets $D_1 u^h(x^{ht}, x^{ht+1})$ be the gradient vector of u^h with respect to the first ℓ coordinates, in general $D_1 u^h(x^{ht}, x^{ht+1}) \neq D_{x^{ht}} u^h(x^{ht}, x^{ht+1})$ since the future planned consumption x^{ht+1} may depend on the current consumption x^{ht} as defined below.

Suppose agent h has taken an action (x^{ht}, m^{ht}) at time t and faces a future environment $(\pi^{t+1}, \bar{x}^{ht+1})$. The decision problem of agent h in period t for period t+1 is to choose $x^{ht+1} \in B^{ht+1}(\pi^{t+1}, y^{ht+1})$ and that $u^h(x^{ht}, x^{ht+1})$ is maximized. Hence a plan associated with an action and an expectation of future events is a correspondence defined by

$$(1) \quad \hat{x}^{ht+1}(x^{ht}, m^{ht}; \pi^{t+1}, \bar{x}^{ht+1})$$

$$= \{x^{ht+1} \in P: u^h(x^{ht}, x^{ht+1}) \text{ is maximized and } x^{ht+1} \in B^{ht+1}(\pi^{t+1}, y^{ht+1})\}$$

for each action $(x^{ht}, m^{ht}) \in P \times R_+$ and $(\pi^{t+1}, \bar{x}^{ht+1}) \in \Pi \times P$.

Corresponding to a plan $\hat{x}^{ht+1}(x^{ht}, m^{ht}; \pi^{t+1}, \bar{x}^{ht+1})$, let

$$\hat{u}^h (x^{ht}, m^{ht}; \pi^{t+1}, \bar{x}^{ht+1}) = u^h(x^{ht}, \hat{x}^{ht+1}(x^{ht}, m^{ht}; \pi^{t+1}, \bar{x}^{ht+1}))$$

be the utility of a plan associated with an action $(x^{ht}, m^{ht}) \in P \times R_+$ and a future event $(\pi^{t+1}, \bar{x}^{ht+1}) \in \Pi \times P$. In order to preserve enough differentiability in the model, a classical assumption on the future market is made for each agent h. That is,

<u>A. 3.</u> $D^2_{x^{ht+1}} u^h(x^{ht}, x^{ht+1})$ is negative definite on the space $\{\mu \in R^\ell : \mu \cdot D_{x^{ht+1}} u^h(x^{ht}, x^{ht+1}) = 0\}$ for every $(x^{ht}, x^{ht+1}) \in P \times P$,

where $D^2_{x^{ht+1}} u^h(x^{ht}, x^{ht+1})$ is a bilinear symmetric form of $u^h(x^{ht}, x^{ht+1})$ with respect to x^{ht+1}. Note, however, that A. 3. is not a concavity hypothesis of u^h on the consequence space usually assumed in the literature. Let

$$\mathscr{U} = \{u^h \in C^k(P \times P, R): k > 2, u^h \text{ is bounded and satisfies A. 2 and A. 3}\} .$$

We call $\mathscr{U}$ the <u>space of direct utility functions</u> from $P \times P$ to R for every agent h. For a classical case of $\mathscr{U}$, we also consider a subspace of direct utility functions denoted by $\mathscr{U}_0$, called the <u>space of classical direct utility functions</u>, i. e.,

$$\mathscr{U}_0 = \Big\{u^h \in \mathscr{U}: \quad D^2 u^h(x^{ht}, x^{ht+1}) \text{ is negative definite on the space } \{\xi \in R^{2\ell}: \xi \cdot Du^h(x^{ht}, x^{ht+1}) = 0\} \text{ for every } (x^{ht}, x^{ht+1}) \in P \times P\Big\} .$$

As we discussed earlier, for any $u^h \in \mathcal{U}$ and $\gamma^h \in \Gamma$, there is a plan $\hat{x}^{ht+1}$ defined by (1) which is an outcome of constrained utility maximization of period $t+1$ conditional to a given action and a future event. By the implicit function theorem, the plan $\hat{x}^{ht+1}(x^{ht}, m^{ht}; \pi^{t+1}, \bar{x}^{ht+1})$ is uniquely defined and $\hat{x}^{ht+1} \in C^{k-1}(P \times R_+ \times \Pi \times P, P)$ with $k > 2$ (see [17], [7], and [23]). In summary, we have the following

PROPOSITION 1. $\hat{x}^{ht+1} \in C^{k-1}(P \times R_+ \times \Pi \times P, P)$ with $k > 2$, where $\hat{x}^{ht+1}$ is defined by (1) for each $u^h \in \mathcal{U}$ and $\gamma^h \in \Gamma$.

II(d) Expected Utility Function

For every $u^h \in \mathcal{U}$ and $\gamma^h \in \Gamma$, if π^t is the price system at time t, the agent's expected utility function of an action (x^{ht}, m^{ht}) is defined by

$$(2) \qquad v^h(x^{ht}, m^{ht}, \pi^t; \gamma^h, u^h) = \int_{\Pi \times P} \hat{u}^h(x^{ht}, m^{ht}; \cdot, \cdot)\, d\gamma^h(\pi^t; \cdot, \cdot) .$$

We observe that the expected utility function v^h defined by (2) depends on money m^{ht} and current price π^t explicitly, which reflects a "generalized real balance effect" (see, for example, [9]). It is important to notice that, in general, v^h is not homogeneous of any degree in m^{ht} and π^t, thus we allow for the possibility of "money illusion" in the expected utility function v^h for every agent h (see, for example, [10] and [13]). We also express in (2) that the expected utility function depends on the economic exogenous data $(\gamma^h, u^h) \in \Gamma \times \mathcal{U}$. Hence v^h is allowed to vary in the product space $\Gamma \times \mathcal{U}$.[4]

[4] For related works see, for example, [13] which considers a similar model with a fixed u^h and γ^h for each agent h and proves the existence of an equilibrium using a standard fixed point argument, and also [5] which holds u^h fixed and allows γ^h to vary to study the continuity of temporary equilibrium in a non-differentiable framework.

For notational convenience, let

$$D_x v^h(x^{ht}, m^{ht}, \pi^t; \gamma^h, u^h) = (\partial v^h(x^{ht}, m^{ht}, \pi^t; \gamma^h, u^h)/\partial x_1^{ht},$$

$$\ldots, \partial v^h(x^{ht}, m^{ht}, \pi^t; \gamma^h, u^h)/\partial x_\ell^{ht}) ,$$

$$D_m v^h(x^{ht}, m^{ht}, \pi^t; \gamma^h, u^h) = \partial v^h(x^{ht}, m^{ht}, \pi^t; \gamma^h, u^h)/\partial m^{ht} , \quad \text{and}$$

$$D_{(x,m)} v^h(x^{ht}, m^{ht}, \pi^t; \gamma^h, u^h) = (D_x v^h(x^{ht}, m^{ht}, \pi^t; \gamma^h, u^h), D_m v^h(x^{ht}, m^{ht}, \pi^t; \gamma^h, u^h))$$

It is clear that

$$D_x v^h(x^{ht}, m^{ht}, \pi^t; \gamma^h, u^h) = \int_{\Pi \times P} D_{x^{ht}} \hat{u}^h (x^{ht}, m^{ht}; \cdot, \cdot)\, d\gamma^h(\pi^t; \cdot, \cdot)$$

and

$$D_m v^h(x^{ht}, m^{ht}, \pi^t; \gamma^h, u^h) = \int_{\Pi \times P} D_{m^{ht}} \hat{u}^h (x^{ht}, m^{ht}; \cdot, \cdot)\, d\gamma^h(\pi^t; \cdot, \cdot)$$

for each $u^h \in \mathscr{U}$ and $\gamma^h \in \Gamma$ because $\operatorname{supp} \gamma^h(\pi^t)$ is compact for each $\pi^t \in \Pi$. The following properties on the expected utility function v^h are easy to establish.

PROPOSITION 2. For each agent h, $v^h(\cdot, \cdot, \cdot; \gamma^h, u^h)$ is continuously differentiable, i.e., $v^h(\cdot, \cdot, \cdot; \gamma^h, u^h) \in C^1(P \times R_+ \times \Pi, R)$ for each $\gamma^h \in \Gamma$ and $u^h \in \mathscr{U}$. In particular, $v^h(\cdot, \cdot, \pi^t; \gamma^h, u^h) \in C^k(P \times R_+, R)$ with $k > 2$ for every $\pi^t \in \Pi$.

PROPOSITION 3. $\overline{v^h(\cdot, m^{ht}, \pi^t; \gamma^h, u^h)^{-1}(c)} \subset P$ for every $\gamma^h \in \Gamma$, $u^h \in \mathscr{U}$, $(m^{ht}, \pi^t) \in R_+ \times \Pi$, and $c \in R$. Moreover, $D_{(x,m)} v^h(x^{ht}, m^{ht}, \pi^t; \gamma^h, u^h) \gg 0$ for each $(x^{ht}, m^{ht}, \pi^t) \in P \times R_+ \times \Pi$.

In view of Proposition 3, we have established the desirability of money although it has no intrinsic value in terms of von Neumann-Morgenstern utility. Finally the existence of a classical expected utility function is presented in the following (see [13] for a proof of the non-differentiable case).

PROPOSITION 4. Given $\pi^t \in \Pi$, if v^h is induced by $u^h \in \mathcal{U}_0$ and $\gamma^h \in \Gamma$, $v^h(\cdot,\cdot,\pi^t;\gamma^h,u^h)$ is a differentiably concave C^{k-1} function from $P \times R_+$ to R with $k > 2$. That is, there exist $\theta \in R^{\ell+1}$ such that the matrix $D^2_{(x,m)}v^h(x^{ht},m^{ht},\pi^t;\gamma^h,u^h)$ is negative definite on the space

$$\{\theta \in R^{\ell+1}: \theta \cdot D_{(x,m)}v^h(x^{ht},m^{ht},\pi^t;\gamma^h,u^h) = 0\}$$

for every action $(x^{ht},m^{ht}) \in P \times R_+$.

Now, the agent's decision problem in period t can be stated as follows: for each $u^h \in \mathcal{U}$ and $\gamma^h \in \Gamma$, if π^t is quoted in period t, the agent facing a future environment $(\pi^{t+1}, \bar{x}^{ht+1})$ will choose an action (x^{ht}, m^{ht}) to optimize the expected utility v^h over the budget set $B^{ht}(\pi^t, y^{ht})$ provided that the plan $\hat{x}^{ht+1}(x^{ht}, m^{ht}; \pi^{t+1}, \bar{x}^{ht+1})$ is realized according to (1).

III. The Space of Money Economies

We are now able to define a space of money economies at period t. First, for each $u^h \in \mathcal{U}$ and $\gamma^h \in \Gamma$ we have an expected utility function v^h defined by (2). Hence the function spaces Γ and $\mathcal{U}$ are important ingredients into the definition of the space of money economies. Moreover, money and commodity endowments in period t are also allowed to vary in the space $P \times R_+$ in addition to varying the γ^h's and u^h's for every agent h. In particular, we do not restrict our analysis to a fixed amount of money supply in the model. Therefore, at time t, all economic characteristics of the model are completely specified by the product space $(\Gamma \times \mathcal{U} \times P \times R_+)^n$. Denote the space of money economies at time t by $\mathcal{E} = (\Gamma \times \mathcal{U} \times P \times R_+)^n$, and a money economy $E = (\gamma, u, \bar{x}, \bar{m})$ is an element of $\mathcal{E}$ where $\gamma = (\gamma^1, \ldots, \gamma^n)$, $u = (u^1, \ldots, u^n)$, $\bar{x} = (\bar{x}^1, \ldots, \bar{x}^n)$ and $\bar{m} = (\bar{m}^1, \ldots, \bar{m}^n)$. In other words, $E \in \mathcal{E}$ is a list of expectations, direct utility functions, commodity and money endowments at time t for all the agents in the model. In particular, $\mathcal{E}_0 = (\Gamma \times \mathcal{U}_0 \times P \times R_+)^n$ is a space of classical money economies. Clearly, $\mathcal{E}$ and $\mathcal{E}_0$ are infinite-dimensional spaces.

In what follows, we will use some notions of differential topology (for example, the Whitney topology on a function space) which will not be explained in this paper. We refer the interested reader to [1], [15] and [19] for the relevant definitions and concepts.

III(a) Topological Structure of the Space of Money Economies

We now need an appropriate topology defined on the space of money economies $\mathcal{E}$, which is the n-fold product of the topologies defined on $\Gamma, \mathscr{U}$, P and R_+, respectively. First, we shall impose a topology on the function space $\mathscr{U} \subset C^k(P \times P, R)$ with a closeness property up to the k-th derivatives. Intuitively, the first topology which comes to mind for $\mathscr{U}$ is the one which is induced by the C^k compact-open topology on $C^k(P \times P, R)$. It is metrizable and the evaluation map defined by a map from $\mathscr{U} \times P \times P$ into R restricted to the compact subset of $P \times P$ is class C^k (see, for instance, [1], page 25 and page 31). Because $P \times P$ is clearly not compact, the induced C^k compact-open topology does not control the behavior of the map u^h "at infinity" very well. For this purpose, the Whitney C^k topology on $C^k(P \times P, R)$ is useful, which is certainly stronger than the C^k compact-open topology and the concept of convergence is even stronger than the C^k uniform convergence. We note that the space $\mathscr{U}$ together with the induced Whitney C^k topology is no longer a topological vector space. Similarly, the topology on Γ can be defined by imposing the C^1 compact-open topology or the Whitney C^1 topology on $C^1(\Pi, \mathscr{M}(\Pi \times P))$ where $\mathscr{M}(\Pi \times P)$ is endowed with the topology of weak convergence.

As noted in the beginning of this subsection, toward studying the "generic" properties of monetary equilibrium, we can now precisely define the topology of the space $\mathscr{E}$ by the n-fold product of the induced Whitney C^1 topology on Γ, the induced Whitney C^k topology on $\mathscr{U}$ and the induced usual topologies on P and R_+, respectively. In what follows, we shall call this product topology of $\mathscr{E}$ the "strong" topology, and omit the time superscript and replace m^{ht-1} by $\overline{m}^h$.

III(b) Two Concepts of Equilibrium

As usual, for every money economy $E = (\gamma, u, \bar{x}, \bar{m}) \in \mathscr{E}$, a short-run monetary equilibrium at the current period is a triple (x, m, π) with

$$\sum_{h=1}^{n} x^h = \sum_{h=1}^{n} \bar{x}^h \quad \text{and} \quad \sum_{h=1}^{n} m^h = \sum_{h=1}^{n} \bar{m}^h ,$$

satisfying $(x^h, m^h) \in B^h(\pi, y^h)$ and that $v^h(x^h, m^h, \pi; \gamma^h, u^h)$ defined by (2) is maximized for every agent h. For any agent h, the Lagrangian condition for (x^h, m^h) to be a critical point of $v^h(\cdot, \cdot, \pi; \gamma^h, u^h)$ subject to $(x^h, m^h) \in B^h(\pi, y^h)$ can be written as $D_{(x,m)} v^h(x^h, m^h, \pi; \gamma^h, u^h) = \lambda^h$. where λ^h is the Lagrangian Multiplier. It is obvious that λ^h depends upon the economic characteristics in the model. To avoid λ^h in the following analysis, we set λ^h at its equilibrium situation for every h, i.e.,

$$\lambda^h = |D_{(x,m)} v^h(x^h, m^h, \pi; \gamma^h, u^h)|$$

where

$$|D_{(x,m)} v^h(x^h, m^h, \pi; \gamma^h, u^h)| = \sum_{k=1}^{\ell} \frac{\partial v^h}{\partial x_k^h}(x^h, m^h, \pi; \gamma^h, u^h) + \frac{\partial v^h}{\partial m^h}(x^h, m^h, \pi; \gamma^h$$

It is obvious that $\lambda^h > 0$ by Proposition 3.

Formally, we define the set of <u>short-run monetary equilibria</u> for $E \in \mathscr{E}$ as

$$W(E) = \Big\{(x,m,\pi)\in P^n\times R^n_+\times \Pi:\ v^h(x^h,m^h,\pi;\gamma^h,u^h) \text{ is maximized},$$

(3)
$$p\cdot x^h + p_0\cdot m^h = p\cdot \bar{x}^h + p_0\cdot \bar{m}^h,\quad h=1,\dots,n,$$

$$\text{and } \sum_{h=1}^n x^h = \sum_{h=1}^n \bar{x}^h,\quad \sum_{h=1}^n m^h = \sum_{h=1}^n \bar{m}^h\Big\}$$

and the set of <u>extended short-run monetary equilibria</u> for $E\in\mathcal{E}$ as

$$\Phi(E) = \Big\{(x,m,\pi)\in P^n\times R^n_+\times \Pi:\ D_{(x,m)}v^h(x^h,m^h,\pi;\gamma^h,u^h)$$

(4)
$$= |D_{(x,m)}v^h(x^h,m^h,\pi;\gamma^h,u^h)|\cdot\pi,\quad p\cdot x^h + p_0\cdot m^h = p\cdot\bar{x}^h + p_0\cdot\bar{m}^h,$$

$$h=1,\dots,n,\quad \text{and } \sum_{h=1}^n x^h = \sum_{h=1}^n \bar{x}^h,\quad \sum_{h=1}^n m^h = \sum_{h=1}^n \bar{m}^h\Big\}$$

We note that the condition $D_m v^h(x^h,m^h,\pi;\gamma^h,u^h) = |D_{(x,m)}v^h(x^h,m^h,\pi;\gamma^h,u^h)|\cdot p_0$ can be obtained from $D_x v^h(x^h,m^h,\pi;\gamma^h,u^h) = |D_{(x,m)}v^h(x^h,m^h,\pi;\gamma^h,u^h)|\cdot p$ and $\Sigma_{j=1}^{\ell} p_j + p_0 = 1$ for each agent h. Furthermore, the admissibility of money $\Sigma_{h=1}^n m^h = \Sigma_{h=1}^n \bar{m}^h$ follows from $p\cdot x^h + p_0\cdot m^h = p\cdot\bar{x}^h + p_0\cdot\bar{m}^h$, $h=1,\dots,n$, $\Sigma_{h=1}^n x^h = \Sigma_{h=1}^n \bar{x}^h$, and $\pi = (p,p_0) \gg 0$. Hence, we rewrite (4) as the following

$$\Phi(E) = \Big\{(x,m,\pi)\in P^n\times R^n_+\times\Pi:\ D_x v^h(x^h,m^h,\pi;\gamma^h,u^h) = |D_{(x,m)}v^h(x^h,m^h,\pi;\gamma^h,u^h)|\cdot p$$

(4')
$$p\cdot x^h + p_0\cdot m^h = p\cdot\bar{x}^h + p_0\cdot\bar{m}^h,\quad h=1,\dots,n,\quad\text{and } \sum_{h=1}^n x^h = \sum_{h=1}^n \bar{x}^h\Big\}$$

For every money economy $E\in\mathcal{E}$, we define a map $\psi_E: P^n\times R^n_+\times\Pi \to R^{\ell n+n+\ell}$ by

$$\psi_E(x,m,\pi)$$

$$(5)\quad = \Big(D_x v^h(x^h, m^h, \pi; \gamma^h, u^h) - |D_{(x,m)} v^h(x^h, m^h, \pi; \gamma^h, u^h)| \cdot p \ ,$$
$$p \cdot x^h + p_0 \cdot m^h - p \cdot \bar{x}^h - p_0 \cdot \bar{m}^h\ , \quad h = 1, \ldots, n\ , \quad \sum_{h=1}^n x^h - \sum_{h=1}^n \bar{x}^h \Big)$$

Obviously, $\psi_E \in C^1(P^n \times R_+^n \times \Pi,\ R^{\ell n + n + \ell})$. From (4') and (5), we have $\Phi(E) = \psi_E^{-1}(0)$ for every money economy $E \in \mathscr{E}$.

PROPOSITION 5. <u>The map</u> $\psi_E: P^n \times R_+^n \times \Pi \to R^{\ell n + n + \ell}$ <u>defined by</u> (5) <u>is proper</u>[5] <u>for every</u> $E \in \mathscr{E}$. <u>In particular</u>, $\Phi(E)$ <u>is a compact subset in</u> $P^n \times R_+^n \times \Pi$ <u>for every</u> $E \in \mathscr{E}$.

<u>Proof.</u> Let $K \subset R^{\ell n + n + \ell}$ be a compact set, then $\psi_E^{-1}(K) = \{(x,m,\pi) \in P^n \times R_+^n \times \Pi:\ D_x v^h(x^h, m^h, \pi; \gamma^h, u^h) + \alpha^h = |D_{(x,m)} v^h(x^h, m^h, \pi; \gamma^h, u^h)| \cdot p,\ \ p \cdot x^h + p_0 \cdot m^h = \beta^h + p \cdot \bar{x}^h + p_0 \cdot \bar{m}^h,$ $h = 1, \ldots, n,\ \ \Sigma_{h=1}^n x^h = \delta + \Sigma_{h=1}^n \bar{x}^h$ for every $k = (\alpha, \beta, \delta) \in K$, where $\alpha = (\alpha^1, \ldots, \alpha^n) \in R^{\ell n}$, $\beta = (\beta^1, \ldots, \beta^n) \in R^n$ and $\delta = (\delta_1, \ldots, \delta_\ell) \in R^\ell\}$ for any $E \in \mathscr{E}$. If $\psi_E^{-1}(K) = \phi$, it is trivial. Suppose $\psi_E^{-1}(K) \neq \phi$, then $\psi_E^{-1}(K) = \psi_E^{-1}(K^*)$ since $\psi_E^{-1}(k) = \phi$ if $k \notin K^*$, where $K^* = \{k = (\alpha, \beta, \delta) \in K:$ $\alpha^h + D_x v^h(x^h, m^h, \pi; \gamma^h, u^h) \gg 0$, $\beta^h + p \cdot \bar{x}^h + p_0 \cdot \bar{m}^h > 0$, $h = 1, \ldots, n$, and $\delta + \Sigma_{h=1}^n \bar{x}^h \gg 0\}$. Furthermore, $\psi_E^{-1}(K)$ is closed in $P^n \times R_+^n \times \Pi$ since ψ_E is class C^1. That is, there is a sequence $\{(x^q, m^q, \pi^q)\}$ with $(x^q, m^q, \pi^q) \in \psi_E^{-1}(K)$ for

---

[5] A continuous mapping f from a topological space X to a topological space Y is called proper if the inverse image of every compact set is compact.

every q such that (x^q, m^q, π^q) converges to $(x^o, m^o, \pi^o) \in \psi_E^{-1}(K)$. It is clear that x^o will not take values on the boundary of the closure of P^n by A. 2(i). Now, we claim $\pi^o \gg 0$. From A. 1, $\mathcal{M}(\Pi \times P)$ is tight (see [3]). That is, there exists an element $\gamma^{ho} \in \mathcal{M}(\Pi \times P)$ such that $\gamma^h(\pi^q)$ converges weakly to γ^{ho}. Without loss of generality, we let $\gamma^{ho} = \gamma^h(\pi^o)$. Consider the expected utility function of the action (x^{ho}, m^{ho}) at π^o,

$$v^h(x^{ho}, m^{ho}, \pi^o; \gamma^h, u^h) = \int_{\Pi \times P} \hat{u}^h(x^{ho}, m^{ho}; \cdot, \cdot)\, d\gamma^h(\pi^o; \cdot, \cdot)$$

which is well defined and class C^{k-1} with $k > 2$ in $(x^{ho}; m^{ho})$. By Propositions 2 and 3, $D_{(x,m)} v^h(x^{ho}, m^{ho}, \pi^o; \gamma^h, u^h) \gg 0$. Since $(x^o, m^o, \pi^o) \in \psi_E^{-1}(K)$, we have

$$D_x v^h(x^{ho}, m^{ho}, \pi^o; \gamma^h, u^h) + \alpha^h = D_{(x,m)} v^h(x^{ho}, m^{ho}, \pi^o; \gamma^h, u^h) | \cdot p^o$$

for each h. This proves $\pi^o \gg 0$. Furthermore, $\psi_E^{-1}(K)$ is bounded by definition. Therefore, $\psi_E^{-1}(K)$ is compact in $P^n \times R_+^n \times \Pi$ for every $E \in \mathcal{E}$. In particular, let $K = \{0\}$, $\Phi(E) = \psi_E^{-1}(0)$ is compact in $P^n \times R_+^n \times \Pi$ for every $E \in \mathcal{E}$.

Q. E. D.

IV. Local Uniqueness and Stability of Short-Run Monetary Equilibrium

In this section we prove local uniqueness and stability of extended short-run monetary equilibrium for "almost all" economies in $\mathscr{E}$, which is defined by a regularity condition on the map ψ_E below. As a corollary we also obtain local uniqueness and stability of short-run monetary equilibrium. The techniques we use are similar to Smale's [23] in which, however, the utility functions are independent of money and price parameters. For local uniqueness, there is no need to assume concavity on the direct utility function.

We first recall a concept of transversality in differential topology. Let Z be a submanifold (see [1] for a definition) of Y, $f \in C^1(X, Y)$ is said to be transversal to Z at x, denoted by $f \pitchfork_x Z$, if either $y = f(x) \notin Z$, or $y = f(x) \in Z$ and $Df(x)[T_x X] + T_y Z = T_y Y$ where $T_x X$ and $T_y Y$ denote the tangent spaces of X at x and Y at y, respectively. If $f \pitchfork_x Z$ for every $x \in X$, $f \pitchfork Z$. Actually, we apply the concept of transversality only in the very special sense of the above. That is, Z is just a single point $\{y\}$, and therefore its tangent space is the zero subspace of $T_y Y$. Thus, f is transversal to y if $Df(x)[T_x X] = T_y Y$ for all $x \in f^{-1}(y)$, which is to say that y is a regular value of f. Now we need a few more definitions. An element $E \in \mathscr{E}$ is called a regular money economy if and only if the associated map ψ_E defined by (5) is transversal to the origin, i.e., $\psi_E \pitchfork 0$. Moreover, the space of regular money economies is denoted by the set $\mathscr{R} = \{E \in \mathscr{E} : \psi_E \pitchfork 0\}$ and the space of classical regular money economies is $\mathscr{R}_0 = \mathscr{R} \cap \mathscr{E}_0$. By a theorem of differential topology (for instance, see [1], p. 45), $\psi_E^{-1}(0) = \Phi(E)$ is a C^1 "submanifold"[6] of the space $P^n \times R_+^n \times \Pi$ for every $E \in \mathscr{R}$. In view of the space of economies $\mathscr{E}$, we have a family of C^1 maps $\psi_E : P^n \times R_+^n \times \Pi \to R^{\ell n+n+\ell}$ defined by (5). In other words, ψ_E is parameterized by the space $\mathscr{E}$. We claim that the subspace of money economies satisfying a transversality requirement (i.e., the space of regular money economies) is open and dense in the "strong" topology defined on the space of economies. Indeed, this set is quite large and the above is a rather strong result. That is, any money economy can be approximated by a regular money economy and any regular money economy is still regular under small perturbation of economic data in the model. Hence, we have

PROPOSITION 6. $\mathscr{R}$ is open and dense in $\mathscr{E}$ with respect to the "strong" topology (defined in III(a)).

Proof. Since P and Π are locally compact, we let $\{K_\alpha\}$ and $\{L_\alpha\}$ be the sequences of compact subsets in P and Π, respectively, such that $K_\alpha \subset K_{\alpha+1}$, $L_\alpha \subset L_{\alpha-1}$ and $P = \bigcup_\alpha K_\alpha$, $\Pi = \bigcup_\alpha L_\alpha$. For each $u^h \in C^k(P \times P, R)$ with $k > 2$, let $u_\alpha^h = u^h | K_\alpha \times K_\alpha \in C^k(K_\alpha \times K_\alpha, R)$. Similar , for each $\gamma^h \in C^1(\Pi, \mathscr{M}(\Pi \times P))$, let $\gamma_\alpha^h = \gamma^h | L_\alpha \in C^1(L_\alpha, \mathscr{M}(\Pi \times P))$. The spaces $C^k(K_\alpha \times K_\alpha, R)$ and $C^1(L_\alpha, \mathscr{M}(\Pi \times P))$ are

[6] Since the space R_+^n is not a manifold nor a manifold with boundary, the notion "submanifold" of R_+^n is defined as follows: let U be an open set of R_+^n in R^n, then a "submanifold" of R_+^n is a subset of R_+^n of the form $V \cap R_+^n$ where V is a submanifold of U.

Banach spaces (see [1], p. 24). Moreover, they are metrizable and separable, hence they are second countable. It is easy to see that the spaces $C^k(P \times P, R)$ and $C^1(\Pi, \mathcal{M}(\Pi \times P))$ are the inverse limits[7] of the sequences $\{C^k(K_a \times K_a, R), f_a\}$ and $\{C^1(L_a, \mathcal{M}(\Pi \times P)), g_a\}$, respectively. That is, $f_\alpha: C^k(K_\alpha \times K_\alpha, R) \to C^k(K_{\alpha-1} \times K_{\alpha-1}, R)$ and $g_\alpha: C^1(L_\alpha, \mathcal{M}(\Pi \times P)) \to C^1(L_{\alpha-1}, \mathcal{M}(\Pi \times P))$ defined by $f_\alpha(u^h_\alpha) = u^h_{\alpha-1} = u^h_\alpha \mid K_{\alpha-1} \times K_{\alpha-1}$ and $g_\alpha(\gamma^h_\alpha) = \gamma^h_{\alpha-1} = \gamma^h_\alpha \mid L_{\alpha-1}$ are continuous. Define

$$\mathcal{U}_\alpha = \{u^h_\alpha \in C^k(K_\alpha \times K_\alpha, R): \text{A.2, A.3 are satisfied}\}$$

and

$$\Gamma_\alpha = \{\gamma^h_\alpha \in C^1(L_\alpha, \mathcal{M}(\Pi \times P)): \text{A.1 is satisfied}\} .$$

Clearly, $\mathcal{U}$ and Γ are the inverse limits of $\{\mathcal{U}_\alpha, f'_\alpha\}$ and $\{\Gamma_\alpha, g'_\alpha\}$, respectively, where $f'_\alpha = f_\alpha \mid \mathcal{U}_\alpha$ and $g'_\alpha = g_\alpha \mid \Gamma_\alpha$. Moreover, let $R_+ = \cup_\alpha M_\alpha$ with M_α compact and $M_\alpha \subset M_{\alpha+1}$, where M_α is constructed in a way such that the corresponding future plan is feasible with respect to the construction of the sequence $\{K_a\}$ in P. That is, given an action in $K_a \times M_a$ and a future event in $\Pi \times P$, the corresponding future plan of every agent is in the compact set K_a, which is computed from the first order condition of utility maximization subject to the budget constraint for the future period (see the expression (1) in II(c)). For each $u^h_a \in \mathcal{U}_a$ and

[7] Let X_a be a topological space and f_a be a continuous map from X_a into X_{a-1} for each index a. The sequence $\{X_a, f_a\}$ is called an inverse limit sequence. The inverse limit space of the sequence $\{X_a, f_a\}$ is a subset of the product $\Pi_a X_a$ such that $f_a(x_a) = x_{a-1}$ for each a and $x_a \in X_a$, $x_{a-1} \in X_{a-1}$.

$\gamma_\alpha^h \in \Gamma_\alpha$, if $\pi \in L_\alpha$ is the current price system, we can define an expected utility function on the compact domain $K_\alpha \times M_\alpha \times L_\alpha$, denoted v_α^h, as follows:

$$v_\alpha^h(x^h, m^h, \pi; \gamma_\alpha^h, u_\alpha^h) = \int_{\Pi \times P} \hat{u}_\alpha^h(x^h, m^h; \cdot, \cdot)\, d\gamma_\alpha^h(\pi; \cdot, \cdot)$$

We need to check that v_a^h depends on γ_a^h, u_a^h in a continuously differentiable fashion. Observe that the evaluation maps of γ_a^h and u_a^h are C^1 and C^k with respect to the induced C^1 and C^k compact-open topologies on Γ_α and $\mathcal{U}_\alpha$, respectively (see [1], p. 25). Hence v_α^h is class C^1.

Let $\mathcal{E}_\alpha = (\Gamma_\alpha \times \mathcal{U}_\alpha \times P \times R_+)^n$, then the space of money economies $\mathcal{E}$ is the inverse limit space of $\{\mathcal{E}_\alpha, F_\alpha\}$ where $F_\alpha : \mathcal{E}_\alpha \to \mathcal{E}_{\alpha-1}$ is defined by

$$F_\alpha = (\underbrace{f'_\alpha, \ldots, f'_\alpha}_{n \text{ times}}, \underbrace{g'_\alpha, \ldots, g'_\alpha}_{n \text{ times}}, \text{id})$$

and id, the identity map, from $P^n \times R_+^n$ to $P^n \times R_+^n$. Define the sequence $\{\mathcal{R}_\alpha, G_\alpha\}$ as $\mathcal{R}_\alpha = \{E_\alpha \in \mathcal{E}_\alpha : \psi_{E_\alpha} \pitchfork 0\}$, $G_\alpha = F_\alpha | \mathcal{R}_\alpha$ and $\psi_{E_\alpha} = \psi_E | K_\alpha^n \times M_\alpha^n \times L_\alpha$. Then $\mathcal{R}$ is the inverse limit of $\{\mathcal{R}_\alpha, G_\alpha\}$. We claim that $\mathcal{R}_\alpha$ is open and dense in $\mathcal{E}_\alpha$ for each α. We apply the transversality density theorem, 19.1 of [1], p. 48. Conditions (1), (2), and (3) of Theorem 19.1 are satisfied. We need to check condition (4) of Theorem 19.1. First, let $\psi_\alpha : \mathcal{E}_\alpha \times K_\alpha^n \times M_\alpha^n \times L_\alpha \to R^{\ell n + n + \ell}$ defined by $\psi_\alpha(E_\alpha, x, m, \pi) = \psi_{E_\alpha}(x, m, \pi)$ for each $E_\alpha \in \mathcal{E}_\alpha$

and $(x, m, \pi) \in K_\alpha^n \times M_\alpha^n \times L_\alpha$ be the evaluation map of ψ_{E_α}. It is clear that ψ_α is class C^1 since v_α^h is class C^1 for each h, and ψ_{E_α} has compact domain for every $E_\alpha \in \mathscr{E}_\alpha$ (for instance, see [1], p. 25). We go on to prove that the evaluation map ψ_α is transversal to 0, i.e., $\psi_{E_\alpha} \pitchfork 0$. By definition, ψ_α is given by

$$\psi_\alpha^h (E_\alpha, x, m, \pi) = \Big(D_x v_\alpha^h (x^h, m^h, \pi; \gamma^h, u^h) - |D_{(x,m)} v_\alpha^h (x^h, m^h, \pi; \gamma^h, u^h)| \cdot p,$$

$$p \cdot x^h + p_0 \cdot m^h - p \cdot \bar{x}^h - p_0 \cdot \bar{m}^h, \quad h = 1, \ldots, n,$$

$$\sum_{h=1}^{n} x^h - \sum_{h=1}^{n} \bar{x}^h \Big)$$

Its derivative at (E_α, x, m, π), i.e.,

$$D\psi_\alpha (E_\alpha, x, m, \pi): T_{(E_\alpha, x, m, \pi)} (\mathscr{E}_\alpha \times K_\alpha^n \times M_\alpha^n \times L_\alpha) \to R^{\ell n + n + \ell}$$

is defined by

$$D\psi_\alpha (E_\alpha, x, m, \pi)(\dot{E}_\alpha, \dot{x}, \dot{m}, \dot{\pi})$$

$$= \Bigg(\frac{\partial^2 v_\alpha^h}{\partial x_k^h \partial E_\alpha} \dot{E}_\alpha - \left(\sum_{i=1}^{\ell} \frac{\partial^2 v_\alpha^h}{\partial x_i^h \partial E_\alpha} + \frac{\partial^2 v_\alpha^h}{\partial m^h \partial E_\alpha} \right) p_k \dot{E}_\alpha$$

$$+ \sum_{j=1}^{\ell} \frac{\partial^2 v_\alpha^h}{\partial x_k^h \partial x_j^h} \dot{x}_j^h - \sum_{j=1}^{\ell} \left(\sum_{i=1}^{\ell} \frac{\partial^2 v_\alpha^h}{\partial x_i^h \partial x_j^h} + \frac{\partial^2 v_\alpha^h}{\partial m^h \partial x_j^h} \right) p_k \dot{x}_j$$

$$+ \frac{\partial^2 v_\alpha^h}{\partial x_k^h \partial m^h} \dot{m}^h - \left(\sum_{i=1}^{\ell} \frac{\partial^2 v_\alpha^h}{\partial x_i^h \partial m^h} + \frac{\partial^2 v_\alpha^h}{\partial m^h \partial m^h} \right) p_k \dot{m}^h$$

$$+ \sum_{j=0}^{\ell} \frac{\partial^2 v_\alpha^h}{\partial x_k^h \partial p_j} \dot{p}_j - \sum_{j=0}^{\ell} \left(\sum_{i=1}^{\ell} \frac{\partial^2 v_\alpha^h}{\partial x_i^h \partial p_j} + \frac{\partial^2 v_\alpha^h}{\partial m^h \partial p_j} \right) p_k \dot{p}_j$$

$$- \left(\sum_{i=1}^{\ell} \frac{\partial v_\alpha^h}{\partial x_i^h} + \frac{\partial v_\alpha^h}{\partial m^h} \right) \dot{p}_k \, , \quad k = 1, \dots, \ell \, , \quad h = 1, \dots, n \, ,$$

$$\dot{p}(\bar{x}^h - x^h) + p(\dot{\bar{x}}^h - \dot{x}^h) + \dot{p}_0(\bar{m}^h - m^h) + p_0(\dot{\bar{m}}^h - \dot{m}^h) \, , \quad h = 1, \dots, n \, ,$$

$$\left. \sum_{h=1}^{n} \dot{\bar{x}}^h - \sum_{h=1}^{n} \dot{x}^h \right) \, ,$$

where $(\dot{E}_\alpha, \dot{x}, \dot{m}, \dot{\pi}) \in T_{(E_\alpha, x, m, \pi)}(\mathscr{E}_\alpha \times K_\alpha^n \times M_\alpha^n \times L_\alpha)$ and $\dot{E}_\alpha = (\dot{\gamma}_\alpha, \dot{u}_\alpha, \dot{\bar{x}}, \dot{\bar{m}})$. Without loss of generality, we take $\dot{E}_\alpha = (0, 0, \dot{\bar{x}}, \dot{\bar{m}})$ and $\dot{x} = 0$, $\dot{m} = 0$. Then

$$D\psi_\alpha(E_\alpha, x, m, \pi)(\dot{E}_\alpha, \dot{x}, \dot{m}, \dot{\pi}) = D\psi_\alpha(E_\alpha, x, m, \pi)((0, 0, \dot{\bar{x}}, \dot{\bar{m}}), 0, 0, \dot{\pi})$$

$$= \left(\sum_{j=0}^{\ell} \frac{\partial^2 v_\alpha^h}{\partial x_k^h \partial p_j} \dot{p}_j - \sum_{j=0}^{\ell} \left(\sum_{i=1}^{\ell} \frac{\partial^2 v_\alpha^h}{\partial x_i^h \partial p_j} + \frac{\partial^2 v_\alpha^h}{\partial m^h \partial p_j} \right) p_k \dot{p}_j \right.$$

$$- \left(\sum_{i=1}^{\ell} \frac{\partial v_\alpha^h}{\partial x_i^h} + \frac{\partial v_\alpha^h}{\partial m^h} \right) \dot{p}_k \, , \quad k = 1, \dots, \ell \, , \quad h = 1, \dots, n \, ,$$

$$\dot{p}\cdot(\bar{x}^h - x^h) + p\cdot\dot{\bar{x}}^h + \dot{p}_0\cdot(\bar{m}^h - m^h) + p_0\cdot\dot{\bar{m}}^h, \quad h = 1,\dots,n, \quad \sum_{h=1}^{n} \dot{\bar{x}}^h \Bigg)$$

For each $(a,b,c) \in R^{\ell n+n+\ell}$ with $a = (a^1,\dots,a^n) \in R^{\ell n}$, $b = (b^1,\dots,b^n) \in R^n$ and $c = (c_1,\dots,c_\ell) \in R^\ell$, there exists $((0,0,\dot{\bar{x}},\dot{\bar{m}}),0,0,\dot{\pi}) \in T_{(E_\alpha,x,m,\pi)}(\mathscr{E}_\alpha \times K_\alpha^n \times M_\alpha^n \times L_\alpha)$ such that

$$D\psi_\alpha(E_\alpha,x,m,\pi)((0,0,\dot{\bar{x}},\dot{\bar{m}}),0,0,\dot{\pi}) = (a,b,c) \quad ,$$

since

$$\sum_{i=1}^{\ell} \frac{\partial v^h}{\partial x_i^h} + \frac{\partial v^h}{\partial m^h} > 0$$

for each h and $\pi \neq 0$. Therefore, $D\psi_\alpha(E_\alpha,x,m,\pi)$ is surjective on $R^{\ell n+n+\ell}$. In particular, $\psi_\alpha \pitchfork 0$. This shows that condition (4) of the transversal density theorem, 19.1 of [1], is satisfied. Hence $\mathscr{R}_\alpha$ is dense in $\mathscr{E}_\alpha$. The openness of $\mathscr{R}_\alpha$ in $\mathscr{E}_\alpha$ follows from the openness of transversal intersection theorem, 18.2 of [1], p. 47.

Let $r_a : \mathscr{E} \to \mathscr{E}_a$ for every a be the canonical restriction maps. To prove that $\mathscr{R}$ is open and dense in $\mathscr{E}$ with respect to the "strong" topology, we first claim that $r_a^{-1}(\mathscr{R}_a)$ is dense in $\mathscr{E}$ with respect to the "strong" topology. We note that r_a is not an open map with respect to the "strong" topology on $\mathscr{E}$. But in fact, we do not need the openness of r_a, and it would suffice if we know that the image of an open set of $\mathscr{E}$ under r_a contains an open set of $\mathscr{E}_a$. Let $N(E) = N^{\epsilon}(u) \times N^{\delta}(\gamma) \times N(\bar{x}, \bar{m})$ be a neighborhood of $E = (u, \gamma, \bar{x}, \bar{m})$ in $\mathscr{E}$ with respect to the "strong" topology, where $N(\bar{x}, \bar{m})$ is an usual neighborhood of $(\bar{x}, \bar{m})$ in $P \times R_+$, $N^{\epsilon}(u) = \{u' \in \mathscr{U}^n : \|D^{\beta}u^h(z) - D^{\beta}u^{h'}(z)\| < \epsilon^h(z)$ for all $z \in P \times P, \beta = 0, 1, \ldots, k$ and $h = 1, \ldots, n\}$ and $N^{\delta}(\gamma) = \{\gamma' \in \Gamma^n : \|D^{\beta}\gamma^h(\pi) - D^{\beta}\gamma^{h'}(\pi)\| < \delta^h(\pi)$ for all $\pi \in \Pi$, $\beta = 0, 1$ and $h = 1, \ldots, n\}$ with $\epsilon^h : P \times P \to R$ and $\delta^h : \Pi \to R$ being positive continuous functions for each h. As we discuss earlier, $\gamma_a(N(E)) \subset \mathscr{E}_a$ is not an open set in general. However, if we shrink $N(E)$ to a neighborhood $N'(E) = N^{\epsilon'}(u) \times N^{\delta}(\gamma) \times N(\bar{x}, \bar{m})$ with $\epsilon^{h'} \leq \epsilon^h$ and $\epsilon^{h'} : P \times P \to R$ is a positive continuous increasing function for every h, it is obvious that for every $E'_a = (u'_a, \gamma'_a, \bar{x}', \bar{m}') \in N'_a(E_a) = N_a^{\epsilon'}(u_a) \times N_a^{\delta}(\gamma_a) \times N(\bar{x}, \bar{m})$, $u_a^{h'}$ can be extended to a function $u^{h'} \in \mathscr{U}$ with $u_a^{h'} = u^{h'} | K_a \times K_a$ and $\gamma_a^{h'}$ can be extended to a function $\gamma^{h'} \in \Gamma$ with $\gamma_a^{h'} = \gamma^{h'} | L_a$ for every h, where $N_a^{\epsilon'}(u_a) = \{u'_a \in \mathscr{U}_a^n : \|D^{\beta}u_a^h(z) - D^{\beta}u_a^{h'}(z)\| < \epsilon^{h'}(z)$ for all $z \in K_a \times K_a, \beta = 0, 1, \ldots, k$ and $h = 1, \ldots, n\}$ and $N_a^{\delta}(\gamma_a) = \{\gamma'_a \in \Gamma_a :$ $\|D^{\beta}\gamma_a^h(\pi) - D^{\beta}\gamma_a^{h'}(\pi)\| < \delta^h(\pi)$ for all $\pi \in L_a$, $\beta = 0, 1$ and $h = 1, \ldots, n\}$. Hence $r_a(N'(E)) = N'_a(E_a)$ is open in $\mathscr{E}_a$ and consequently $r_a(N(E))$ contains an open set. Together with the fact that $\mathscr{R}_a$ is dense in $\mathscr{E}_a$, we have $r_a(N(E)) \cap \mathscr{R}_a \neq \phi$. This means that there exists an $E' \in N(E)$ such that $r_a(E') \in \mathscr{R}_a$ or $E' \in r_a^{-1}(\mathscr{R}_a)$. Hence $N(E) \cap r_a^{-1}(\mathscr{R}_a) \neq \phi$, or equivalently $r_a^{-1}(\mathscr{R}_a)$ is dense in $\mathscr{E}$. By definition, $\mathscr{R} = \bigcap_a r_a^{-1}(\mathscr{R}_a)$. Therefore, $\mathscr{R}$ is dense in $\mathscr{E}$ with respect to the "strong" topology since $\mathscr{E}$ is a Baire space. Moreover, if $E \in \mathscr{R}$, then by definition, $E_a \in \mathscr{R}_a$ with $G_a(E_a) = E_{a-1}$ for each a. Since $\mathscr{R}_a$ is open in $\mathscr{E}_a$, there exists a neighborhood $N_a(E_a) = N_a^{\epsilon}(u_a) \times N_a^{\delta}(\gamma_a) \times N(\bar{x}, \bar{m})$ of E_a in $\mathscr{E}_a$ with

$N_\alpha(E_\alpha) \subset \mathscr{R}_\alpha$ for each α. In particular, $N_\alpha^\epsilon(u_\alpha) = \{u'_\alpha \in \mathscr{U}_\alpha^n :$ $\|D^\beta u_\alpha^h(z) - D^\beta u_\alpha^{h'}(z)\| < \epsilon_\alpha^h(z)$ for every $z \in K_\alpha \times K_\alpha$, $\beta = 0, 1, \ldots, k$ and $h = 1, \ldots, n\}$ and $N_\alpha^\delta(\gamma_\alpha) = \{\gamma'_\alpha \in \Gamma_\alpha^n : \|D^\beta \gamma_\alpha^h(\pi) - D^\beta \gamma_\alpha^{h'}(\pi)\| < \delta_\alpha^h(\pi)$ for every $\pi \in L_\alpha$, $\beta = 0, 1$ and $h = 1, \ldots, n\}$, where $\epsilon_\alpha^h : K_\alpha \times K_\alpha \to R$ and $\delta_\alpha^h : L_\alpha \to R$ are positive continuous functions, respectively, for each h. We now choose a positive continuous function $\delta^h : \Pi \to R$ with $\delta_\alpha^h = \delta^h | L_\alpha$ and a positive continuous function $\epsilon^{h'} : P \times P \to R$ with $\epsilon^{h'}(z) \le \epsilon_\alpha^h(z)$ for every $z \in K_\alpha \times K_\alpha$ and all α. Then $N'(E) = N^{\epsilon'}(u) \times N^\delta(\gamma) \times N(\bar{x}, \bar{m})$ is a neighborhood of E in $\mathscr{E}$ and $N'(E) \subset \mathscr{R}$. Hence the openness of $\mathscr{R}$ in $\mathscr{E}$ follows. Q. E. D.

We now prove the stability theorem.

THEOREM 1. <u>The extended short-run monetary equilibrium correspondence Φ defined by (4) or (4') is continuous on $\mathscr{R}$, i.e., $\Phi(E)$ is stable for every $E \in \mathscr{R}$ with respect to the "strong" topology.</u>

<u>Proof.</u> For every regular money economy $E \in \mathscr{R}$, we have $\psi_E \pitchfork 0$. By the openness property of $\mathscr{R}$ in $\mathscr{E}$, $\psi_{E'} \pitchfork 0$ for $E' \in \mathscr{R}$ near E. We claim that for E' near E, $\psi_{E'}^{-1}(0)$ and $\psi_E^{-1}(0)$ are close to each other, i.e., the extended temporary monetary equilibrium correspondence restricted to the space of regular money economies is continuous. It has been proven in Proposition 6 that with the "strong" topology defined on $\mathscr{E}$, the evaluation map ψ_α defined by $\psi_\alpha(E_\alpha, x, m, \pi) = \psi_{E_\alpha}(x, m, \pi)$ is class C^1. Moreover, for every $E_\alpha \in \mathscr{R}_\alpha$, ψ_{E_α} is a C^1 local diffeomorphism by the inverse function theorem since

$$D\psi_{E_\alpha}(x,m,\pi):\ T_{(x,m,\pi)}(K^n_\alpha \times M^n_\alpha \times L_\alpha) \to R^{\ell n+n+\ell}$$

with $(x,m,\pi) \in \psi^{-1}_{E_\alpha}(0)$, is an isomorphism. Hence the stability property of the map $\Phi_\alpha = \Phi \mid \mathscr{R}_\alpha : \mathscr{R}_\alpha \to P^n \times R^n_+ \times \Pi$ follows by an application of the implicit function theorem on the evaluation map ψ_α. That is, there exist neighborhoods $N_a(E_a)$ of $E_a \in \mathscr{R}_a$ and V of $(x,m,\pi) \in K^n_a \times M^n_a \times L_a \subset P^n \times R^n_+ \times \Pi$, and a C^1 function $\xi_a : N_a(E_a) \to V$ such that $\psi_\alpha(E'_\alpha, \xi_\alpha(E'_\alpha)) = 0$ for every $E'_\alpha \in N_\alpha(E_a)$ and $\xi_\alpha(E_\alpha) = (x,m,\pi)$. Since $\Phi_{\alpha-1}(E_{\alpha-1}) \subset \Phi_\alpha(E_\alpha)$ for each α, we have the following diagram

$$\begin{array}{ccc} N_{a-1}(E_{a-1}) & \xleftarrow{\;G_\alpha \mid N_\alpha(E_a)\;} & N_\alpha(E_a) \\ \downarrow{\scriptstyle \xi_{\alpha-1}} & & \downarrow{\scriptstyle \xi_\alpha} \\ V & \xleftarrow{\;\text{id}\;} & V \end{array}$$

which is commutative, i.e., $\xi_{\alpha-1} \circ G_\alpha | N_a(E_a) = \text{id} \circ \xi_\alpha$ for each α. This implies that at the inverse limit there is a continuous function $\xi: N'(E) \to V$ such that $\psi(E', \xi(E')) = 0$ for every $E' \in N'(E)$ and $\xi(E) = (x,m,\pi)$ where $N'(E)$ is a neighborhood as constructed in the proof of Proposition 6. Hence the extended equilibrium correspondence Φ is stable for every $E \in \mathscr{R}$ with respect to the "strong" topology. Q. E. D.

COROLLARY 1. The short-run monetary equilibrium correspondence restricted to the space of classical regular money economies is continuous. That is, $W(E)$ defined by (3) is stable for every $E \in \mathscr{R}_0$ with respect to the "strong" topology.

Proof. Consider the map $\psi_E: P^n \times R^n_+ \times \Pi \to R^{\ell n+n+\ell}$ defined by (5) and suppose $m^h = (p/p_0)\cdot(\bar{x}^h - x^h) + \bar{m}^h$ for every agent h. This can be done since $p_0 > 0$. Define

$$\psi_E^*(x,\pi) = \psi_E\left(x,\ (p/p_0)\cdot(\bar{x}^h - x^h) + \bar{m}^h,\ h = 1,\ldots,n,\pi\right)$$

for any $x \in P^n$, $\pi \in \Pi$ and $(p/p_0)\cdot(\bar{x}^h - x^h) + \bar{m}^h = m^h \geq 0$. Let $\Phi^*(E)$ and $W^*(E)$ be the projection of $\Phi(E)$ and $W(E)$ on $P^n \times \Pi$, respectively. It is clear that $W^*(E) \subset \Phi^*(E) = \psi_E^{*-1}(0)$ for every $E \in \mathscr{E}$ and $W^*(E) = \Phi^*(E) = \psi_E^{*-1}(0)$ for every $E \in \mathscr{E}_0$. By Theorem 1, $\Phi(E)$ is continuous for every $E \in \mathscr{R}$ with respect to the "strong" topology given on $\mathscr{E}$, and hence, so is $\Phi^*(E)$. This proves that $W^*(E)$ is continuous for every $E \in \mathscr{R}_0$ with respect to the "strong" topology. By Definition (3) we can write

$$W(E) = \left\{(x,m,\pi) \in P^n \times R^n_+ \times \Pi:\ m^h = (p/p_0)\cdot(\bar{x}^h - x^h) + \bar{m}^h,\right.$$

$$\left. h = 1,\ldots,n \ \text{ and } \ (x,\pi) \in W^*(E)\right\}.$$

The corollary follows. Q. E. D.

Finally, we prove local uniqueness of the extended short-run monetary equilibria for an open and dense subset $\mathscr{R}$ of the space of all money economies $\mathscr{E}$. Since the extended monetary equilibrium correspondence is compact-valued for every $E \in \mathscr{E}$ (Proposition 5), the finiteness of equilibria clearly follows from the local uniqueness.

THEOREM 2. For every regular money economy $E \in \mathscr{R}$, the extended short-run monetary equilibria are locally unique.

Proof. Since $\Phi(E) = \psi_E^{-1}(0)$ for every $E \in \mathscr{E}$ and $\dim \psi_E^{-1}(0) = \dim (P^n \times R_+^n \times \Pi) - \dim R^{\ell n+n+\ell} = 0$ if 0 is a regular value of the map ψ_E, or equivalently, if $E \in \mathscr{R}$. Thus $\psi_E^{-1}(0)$ is a submanifold with zero dimension for every $E \in \mathscr{R}$. Hence $\Phi(E)$ defined by (4) or (4') is a discrete set. Q.E.D.

COROLLARY 2. For every regular money economy $E \in \mathscr{R}$, the short-run monetary equilibria are locally unique.

Proof. In view of the proof of Corollary 1, $W^*(E) \subset \Phi^*(E) = \psi_E^{*-1}(0)$ for every $E \in \mathscr{E}$. By Theorem 2, $\psi_E^{-1}(0)$ is a discrete set, and hence so is $\psi_E^{*-1}(0)$ for every $E \in \mathscr{R}$. This shows that the set $W^*(E)$ is also discrete for every $E \in \mathscr{R}$. Q.E.D.

V. Existence of Short-Run Monetary Equilibrium

Although the extended (or classical) short-run monetary equilibria are locally unique for each regular money economy E, it is possible that $\Phi(E)$ or $W(E)$ is an empty set. It is known ([13], [25]) that there exists monetary equilibrium for the economies with continuous, concave, monotone direct utility functions and with a compactness requirement on the expectations. In other words $W(E) \neq \phi$ for every $E \in \mathscr{E}_0$. In this section, we provide a different proof of $W(E) \neq \phi$ for every $E \in \mathscr{E}_0$ in the differentiable framework. We first prove the following.

PROPOSITION 7. There exists a classical regular money economy with unique short-run monetary equilibrium.

Proof. We prove this proposition by considering a nonempty subset $\mathscr{U}_0$ for each agent, which contains interperiod additive separable utility functions, denoted by $\mathscr{U}_{S0} \subset \mathscr{U}_0 \subset \mathscr{U}$. Define $\mathscr{E}_{S0} = (\Gamma \times \mathscr{U}_{S0} \times P \times R_+)^n$, then $\mathscr{E}_{S0} \subset \mathscr{E}_0 \subset \mathscr{E}$. For an $E = (\gamma, u, \bar{x}, \bar{m}) \in \mathscr{E}_{S0}$, let $(\bar{x}, \bar{m})$ be an equilibrium allocation (this is possible if we choose $E = (\gamma, u, \bar{x}, \bar{m})$ with $\gamma^1 = \cdots = \gamma^n$, $u^1 = \cdots = u^n$, $\bar{x}^1 = \cdots = \bar{x}^n$, $\bar{m}^1 = \cdots = \bar{m}^n$). Then there exists a unique $\pi^* \in \Pi$ such that $\psi_E(\bar{x}, \bar{m}, \pi^*) = 0$ since $\gamma^h \in \Gamma$ and $u^h \in \mathscr{U}_0$ for every h. In particular,

$$D_x v^h(\bar{x}^h, \bar{m}^h, \pi^*; \gamma^h, u^h) = |D_{(x,m)} v^h(\bar{x}^h, \bar{m}^h, \pi^*; \gamma^h, u^h)| \cdot p^*$$

for every agent h. Since $u^h \in \mathscr{U}_{S0}$, v^h is differentiably concave by Proposition 4 and additively separable with respect to x^h and (m^h, π).

By a well known result of consumer theory on convex preferences or concave utilities (for instance, see [22]), $p^* \cdot x^h + p_0^* \cdot m^h > p^* \cdot \bar{x}^h + p_0^* \cdot \bar{m}^h$ for every h with $(\bar{x}^h, \bar{m}^h) \neq (x^h, m^h)$ and $\psi_E(x, m, \pi^*) = 0$. This is self contradictory. Hence, $(\bar{x}, \bar{m}, \pi^*)$ is a unique equilibrium for the economy E. Furthermore, the derivative matrix of ψ_E has rank $\ell n + n + \ell$ at $(\bar{x}, \bar{m}, \pi^*)$. This follows from the facts that for every agent h, v^h is additively separable in x^h and (m^h, π), $D_{(x,m)} v^h(\bar{x}^h, \bar{m}^h, \pi^*; \gamma^h, u^h) >> 0$, and $D^2_{(x,m)} v^h(\bar{x}^h, \bar{m}^h, \pi^*; \gamma^h, u^h)$ is negative definite on the space $\{\theta \in R^{\ell+1} : \theta \cdot D_{(x,m)} v^h(\bar{x}^h, \bar{m}^h, \pi^*; \gamma^h, u^h) = 0\}$. Hence $E = (\gamma, u, \bar{x}, \bar{m}) \in \mathscr{R}$. Q.E.D.

As a matter of fact, the "strong" topology defined on $\mathscr{E}$, which establishes the generic local uniqueness and stability of extended (or classical) short-run monetary equilibrium, does not make the space $\mathscr{E}$ a topological vector space since $P^n \times R^n_+ \times \Pi$ is certainly non-compact. Toward proving the existence theorem, we need the so-called "weak" topology of $\mathscr{E}$ defined by the n-fold product of the induced C^1 compact-open topology on Γ, the induced C^k compact-open topology on $\mathscr{U}$ and the induced usual topologies on P and R_+, respectively. It is obvious that the "weak" topology on $\mathscr{E}$ does not control the behavior of the maps and their derivatives "at infinity" very well, but it would make $\mathscr{E}$ metrizable. We now prove an existence theorem.

THEOREM 3. <u>There exists extended short-run monetary equilibrium for every money economy, i.e., for all</u> $E \in \mathscr{E}$, $\Phi(E) \neq \phi$.

Proof. First, we check $\mathscr{E}$ is arcwise connected.[8] Let $E, E' \in \mathscr{E}$. We construct $E^\tau = \tau E + (1-\tau)E'$ for $\tau \in [0,1]$, i.e.,

$$E^\tau = (\gamma^\tau, u^\tau, \bar{x}^\tau, \bar{m}^\tau) = \left(\tau\gamma + (1-\tau)\gamma', \ \tau u + (1-\tau)u', \ \tau\bar{x} + (1-\tau)\bar{x}', \ \tau\bar{m} + (1-\tau)\bar{m}'\right)$$

By the "weak" topology given on $\mathscr{E}$, $\gamma^{h\tau} \in C^1(\Pi, \mathscr{M}(\Pi \times P))$, $u^{h\tau} \in C^k(P \times P, R)$ with $k > 2$, $\bar{x}^{h\tau} \in P$ and $\bar{m}^{h\tau} \in R_+$ for every h. It is easy to see that $u^{h\tau}$ is bounded and satisfies A. 2 and A. 3. That is, $u^{h\tau} \in \mathscr{U}$. Moreover, we recall that the support of a measure (probability measure as a special case) can be written in the following form: $\operatorname{supp} \gamma^h(\pi) = \{z \in \Pi \times P: \gamma^h(\pi; N) > 0$ for each open set N containing $z\}$ (see [20], Theorem 2. 1), where z is a pair of future prices and future endowments. We claim that (i) $\operatorname{supp} \gamma^h(\pi) = \operatorname{supp} \alpha\gamma^h(\pi)$ for $\alpha > 0$, and (ii) $\operatorname{supp}(\gamma^h(\pi) + \gamma^{h'}(\pi)) \subset \operatorname{supp} \gamma^h(\pi) \cup \operatorname{supp} \gamma^{h'}(\pi)$ for any $\pi \in \Pi$. (i) is clear. If $z \in \operatorname{supp}(\gamma^h(\pi) + \gamma^{h'}(\pi))$, $\gamma^h(\pi; N) + \gamma^{h'}(\pi; N) > 0$ for every open set N containing z. That is, we have either $\gamma^h(\pi; N) > 0$ or $\gamma^{h'}(\pi; N) > 0$ for every open set N containing z. This implies $z \in \operatorname{supp} \gamma^h(\pi) \cup \operatorname{supp} \gamma^{h'}(\pi)$. Therefore, $\operatorname{supp}(\gamma^h(\pi) + \gamma^{h'}(\pi)) \subset \operatorname{supp} \gamma^h(\pi) \cup \operatorname{supp} \gamma^{h'}(\pi)$ for any $\pi \in \Pi$. We recall that $\gamma^{h\tau} = \tau\gamma^h + (1-\tau)\gamma^{h'}$ with $\tau \in [0,1]$. If $\tau = 0$, then $\gamma^{h\tau} = \gamma^{h'}$ and $\operatorname{supp} \gamma^{h\tau}(\pi) = \operatorname{supp} \gamma^{h'}(\pi)$ for any $\pi \in \Pi$. Similarly, if $\tau = 1$, $\operatorname{supp} \gamma^{h\tau}(\pi) = \operatorname{supp} \gamma^h(\pi)$ for any $\pi \in \Pi$. If $0 < \tau < 1$,

$$\begin{aligned} \operatorname{supp} \gamma^{h\tau}(\pi^t) &= \operatorname{supp}(\tau\gamma^h(\pi) + (1-\tau)\gamma^{h'}(\pi)) \subset \operatorname{supp} \tau\gamma^h(\pi) + \operatorname{supp}(1-\tau)\gamma^{h'}(\pi) \\ &= \operatorname{supp} \gamma^h(\pi) \cup \operatorname{supp} \gamma^{h'}(\pi) \end{aligned}$$

---

[8] A topological space X is said to be arcwise-connected if, for each pair of points a, b in X, there exists a path in X with origin a and end point b, where a path in X is a continuous function $f: [0,1] \to X$ such that $f(0) = a$, $f(1) = b$ (see also [19]).

for any $\pi \in \Pi$. Since $\gamma^h, \gamma^{h'} \in \Gamma$ for every agent h, $\operatorname{supp} \gamma^h(\pi)$ and $\operatorname{supp} \gamma^{h'}(\pi)$ are compact for any $\pi \in \Pi$. Hence $\operatorname{supp} \gamma^{h\tau}(\pi)$ is a compact set in $\Pi \times P$ for $\pi \in \Pi$ and $\tau \in [0, 1]$. In other words, $\gamma^{h\tau} \in \Gamma$. This proves that $E^\tau = (\gamma^\tau, u^\tau, \bar{x}^\tau, \bar{m}^\tau) \in \mathscr{E}$. Now, consider the map $\psi_E: P^n \times R^n_+ \times \Pi \to R^{\ell n+n+\ell}$ defined by (5) and let $m^h = (p/p_0)\cdot(\bar{x}^h - x^h) + \bar{m}^h$ for every agent h. This, in fact, can be done since $p_0 > 0$. Define the C^1 map $\psi^*_E: P^n \times \Pi \to R^{\ell n+\ell}$ such that

$$\psi^*_E(x,\pi) = \psi_E\left(x, \frac{p}{p_0}\cdot(\bar{x}^h - x^h) + \bar{m}^h, \; h = 1, \ldots, n, \; \pi\right)$$

and $(p/p_0)\cdot(\bar{x}^h - x^h) + \bar{m}^h \geq 0$. It is clear that $\psi_E(x, (p/p_0)\cdot(\bar{x}^h - x^h) + \bar{m}^h, h = 1, \ldots, n, \pi) = 0$ if and only if $\psi^*_E(x,\pi) = 0$. From Proposition 5, the Brouwer degree of the map ψ^*_E is defined. If $E \in \mathscr{R}$, the degree of the map ψ^*_E is equal to the algebraic sum of the orientations of the elements of $\psi^{*-1}_E(0)$. Let $\deg \psi^*_E$ denote the degree of map ψ^*_E. By Proposition 7, there exists $E \in \mathscr{R} \subset \mathscr{E}$, $\deg \psi^*_E$ is one. Finally, the Brouwer degree is homotopy invariant,[9] so that $\deg \psi^*_E$ is one for every $E \in \mathscr{E}$. This implies $\psi^{*-1}_E(0) \neq \phi$ and hence $\Phi(E) = \psi^{-1}_E(0) \neq \phi$ for every $E \in \mathscr{E}$. Q. E. D.

---

[9] Two mappings $f, g: X \to Y$ are homotopic if there exists a continuous map $F: X \times [0, 1] \to Y$ with $F(x, 0) = f(x)$ and $f(x, 1) = g(x)$ for all $x \in X$. To say that Brouwer degree is homotopy invariant is equivalent to saying that any homotopic maps have the same Brouwer degree. (See also, [19].)

COROLLARY 3. For every classical money economy, there is a short-run monetary equilibrium, i.e., $W(E) \neq \phi$ for all $E \in \mathscr{E}_0$.

Proof. This follows from the relationship that $W^*(E) = \Phi^*(E) = \psi_E^{*-1}(0)$ for every $E \in \mathscr{E}_0$, and the definition

$$W(E) = \left\{(x, m, \pi) \in P^n \times R_+^n \times \Pi : m^h = \frac{p}{p_0} \cdot (\bar{x}^h - x^h) + \bar{m}^h, \quad h = 1, \ldots, n, \right.$$

$$\left. \text{and} \quad (x, \pi) \in W^*(E) \right\} .$$

Q. E. D.

REFERENCES

1. Abraham, R. and J. Robbin, Transversal Mappings and Flows, W.A. Benjamin, Inc., New York, 1967.

2. Arrow, K.J. and F.H. Hahn, General Competitive Analysis, Holden-Day, San Francisco, 1971.

3. Billingsley, P., Convergence of Probability Measures, Wiley, 1968.

4. Chichilnisky, G. and P.J. Kalman, "Special Properties of Critical Points and Operators of Parametrized Manifolds in Economics", Journal of Mathematical Analysis and Applications, Feb. 1977.

5. Christiansen, D.S. and M. Majumdar, "On Shifting Temporary Equilibrium", Department of Economics, Cornell University, 1974.

6. Debreu, G., "Economies with a Finite Set of Equilibria", Econometrica 38, 1970, pp. 387-392.

7. Debreu, G., "Smooth Preferences", Econometrica 40, 1972, pp. 603-615.

8. Dudley, R. M., "Convergence of Baire Measures," Studia Mathematica 27, 1966, pp. 251-268.

9. Dusansky, R. and P.J. Kalman, "The Real Balance Effect and the Traditional Theory of Consumer Behavior: A Reconciliation", Journal of Economic Theory 5, 1972, pp. 336-347.

10. Dusansky, R. and P.J. Kalman, "The Foundations of Money Illusion in a Neoclassical Micro-Monetary Model", American Economic Review LXIV, March 1974, pp. 115-122.

11. Fuchs, G., "Asymptotic Stability of Stationary Temporary Equilibria and Changes in Expectations," Journal of Economic Theory, 13, 1976, pp. 201-216.

12. Fuchs, G. and G. Laroque, "Dynamics of Temporary Equilibria and Expectations", Econometrica, 44, 1976, pp. 1157-1178.

13. Grandmont, J.-M., "On the Short-Run Equilibrium in a Monetary Economy", in J. Drezé (ed.), Allocation Under Uncertainty: Equilibrium and Optimality, Macmillan, New York, 1974, pp. 213-228.

14. Hicks, J., Value and Capital, Clarendon Press, 1946.

15. Hirsch, M.W., Notes on Differential Topology, Department of Mathematics, University of California, Berkeley, 1973.

16. Hool, R. B., "Temporary Walrasian Equilibrium in a Monetary Economy," in Adaptive Economic Models, R. H. Day and T. Groves (eds.), Academic Press, New York, 1975, pp. 499-512.

17. Katzner, D. W., "A Note on the Differentiability of Consumer Demand Functions", Econometrica 36, 1968, pp. 415-418.

18. Lin, Kuan-Pin, "On Temporary Monetary Equilibrium Theory: A Differentiable Approach", Ph. D. thesis, SUNY at Stony Brook, 1977.

19. Milnor, J., Topology from a Differentiable Viewpoint, University of Virginia Press, 1965.

20. Parthasarathy, K. R., Probability Measures on Metric Space, Academic Press, 1967.

21. Patinkin, D., Money, Interest and Price, Harper and Row, 1965.

22. Samuelson, P. A., The Foundations of Economic Analysis, Harvard University Press, Cambridge, Mass., 1947.

23. Smale, S., "Global Analysis and Economics IIA: Extensions of a Theorem of Debreu", Journal of Mathematical Economics 1, 1974, pp. 1-14.

24. Smale, S., "Global Analysis and Economics IV: Finiteness and Stability of Equilibria with General Consumption Sets and Production", Journal of Mathematical Economics 1, 1974, pp. 119-127.

25. Sondermann, D., "Temporary Competitive Equilibrium Under Uncertainty", in J. Dreze (ed.), Allocation Under Uncertainty: Equilibrium and Optimality, Macmillan, New York, 1974, pp. 229-253.

26. Stigum, B. P., "Competitive Equilibria under Uncertainty", Quarterly Journal of Economics 83, 1969, pp. 533-561.

27. Wallace, A. H., Algebraic Topology: Homology and Cohomology, Benjamin, New York, 1970.

28. Younès, Y., "Money and Interest in a Walrasian Short-Run Equilibrium", MSSB Working Paper, University of California, Berkeley, 1973.

A Differentiable Temporary Equilibrium Theory*

by

Peter J. Kalman and Kuan-Pin Lin
Department of Economics
Harvard University

July 1976

*This work was supported in part by the Urban Institute, Washington, D.C. P. J. Kalman is visiting Harvard from SUNY at Stony Brook. We thank K. J. Arrow and M. W. Hirsch for helpful comments.

In two recent papers G. Debreu [6] and S. Smale [18] gave illuminating discussions of the application of differential topology to the area of general Walrasian equilibrium analysis. In particular, Smale pointed out a weakness of the Walrasian theory, also commonly referred to as the "Arrow-Debreu Theory." This weakness refers to the "reliance of the theory on long range optimization" where "economic agents make one life-long decision, optimizing some value." Moreover, "with future dating of commodities, time has almost an artificial role." Another weakness of the Arrow-Debreu theory is that monetary phenomena cannot adequately be studied in that model and hence, a micro-foundation for monetary theory is not available in that framework. These weaknesses can be eliminated by allowing sequential decision making according to the agents' expectations of future circumstances. This paper discusses the extension of Arrow-Debreu theory to this sequential setting within a differentiable framework applying tools of differential topology.

The differential topology approach to equilibrium theory originates with the work of Debreu [4] and is followed up by the works of E. and H. Dierker [7] and Smale [17] among others. This approach allows one to directly study equilibrium properties such as existence, local uniqueness, stability, rate of convergence of the core of an economy and the equivalence of the Pareto optimum and the equilibrium allocation (see Debreu [6] for an excellent discussion of these concepts). In this paper, we consider short run or temporary equilibrium in a Walrasian setting from this differentiable viewpoint which originates with the present authors work in [14]. The basic idea of the temporary equilibrium model is that each agent's decisions are made sequentially and may be revised as time progresses according to the information conveyed about the future environment, which is based upon the agent's knowledge of the past. "Loosely speaking, whereas the Arrow-Debreu analysis is essentially static, the short-run equilibrium analysis studies the dynamic features of the economy within a short time interval [19]." In the temporary equilibrium approach, agent's expectations of future information are taken as data of the economic system. These expectations link the subsequent spot markets together and play the most important role in determining the equilibrium properties where the information specifying the future environment is uncertain. The idea of temporary equilibrium can be traced back to the work of Hicks [12] and was used by Patinkin [16] in his integration of monetary and value theories. This idea is also very much part of the Keynesian thinking. More recent contributions to formal temporary equilibrium models can be found in the works of Stigum [20], Arrow and Hahn [1], Grandmont [10], J. Green [11] and Sondermann [19] among others. These authors work in a nondifferentiable framework and study conditions for existence of temporary equilibrium by using standard fixed point theorems.

As pointed out by Debreu [4], once there is a general solution to the existence problem, one should investigate the structure of the set of equilibria. Otherwise, the explanation of equilibrium is totally indeterminate. First, there may exist infinitely many equilibria. Also, the economic system may be unstable in the sense that a small change of economic data would lead to an entirely different set of equilibria. Therefore, it is highly desirable to have an economy for which the set of equilibria is locally unique (i.e., discrete) and stable (i.e., continuous). These properties are also needed if one wants to study the comparative statics of the system. In the following, using tools of differential topology, we study local uniqueness, stability and also existence of temporary equilibrium in a pure exchange model (for a more formal treatment of this model and also for the formal proofs of the results see [14]).

In a temporary equilibrium model, the strategy of an agent's decision making at present involves making a consumption plan for the future which in general is influenced by an uncertain environment. To specify a subjective uncertainty about the future environment for each agent, one assumes that each agent forecasts future events which take the form of a probability distribution. In general, this forecast depends on current and past information. Let γ^h be the probability assigned to the occurrence of future events for agent h. We will employ three assumptions on γ^h. First, we assume that the sequence $\{\gamma_q^h\}$ converges weakly to γ^h. This means that the probabilities γ_q^h and γ^h must satisfy the condition that the integral $\int f d\gamma_q^h$ converges to $\int f d\gamma^h$ for every bounded, continuous real function f on the future environment. Secondly, we have to restrict the smallest closed set in the space of future environments to be compact with probability one of occurrence. Economically, this means that the change of the expectations of future events are inelastic with respect to the current observations. Finally, we assume γ^h is continuously differentiable, also called class C^1. This last assumption is needed for applying the tools of differential topology.[1] For each agent h, let Γ be the family of expectations γ^h satisfying the three assumptions above.

We now discuss the utility functions involved in the temporary equilibrium model. As usual, each agent's intertemporal preferences can be represented by a von Neumann-Morgenstern utility function u^h which is a bounded, continuous real valued function from the space of consumption streams over periods to the real line. We assume that each agent's utility function u^h is k times

---

[1]This assumption is not unreasonable at all since the approximation theorems ensure that any continuous function can be closely approximated by a differentiab function.

continuously differentiable, i.e. class C^k, $k>2$. We also assume that u^h is a monotone increasing function with respect to current and future consumption streams and concave with respect to future consumption streams only. That is, the "Hessian" is negative definite for small disturbance along the contour of u^h with respect to future consumption. Note that the concavity hypothesis on u^h is not assumed on the spaces of consumption streams over all periods, which is usually assumed in the literature. For notational convenience, let U be the family of utility functions u^h satisfying the above assumptions for each agent h. The decision problem facing agent h in the current period for his/her future consumption stream, is to make a plan which maximizes u^h and satisfies the future budget constraints.

For each γ^h in Γ and u^h in U, the consumption plan for the future is a $(k-1)$ times continuously differentiable function with $k > 2$. This fact follows directly from the implicit function theorem. For each agent h, given a von Neumann-Morgenstern utility function u^h in U and an expectation γ^h in Γ, we can define his/her expected utility function

$$v^h = \int u^h \, d\,\gamma^h$$

over the future events. Clearly, the expected utility function v^h depends on γ^h in Γ and u^h in U. This means that changes of views or beliefs of the future environment and changes in tastes are capable of influencing the present situation which is represented by the expected utility function v^h.

For a particular case of two periods, t and $t+1$, let the vectors x^{ht}, x^{ht+1} be the consumption of agent h in periods t and $t+1$ respectively. The pair (x^{ht}, x^{ht+1}) is the consumption stream over the two periods and m^{ht} is his money holding at time t. At the beginning of period t, every agent h knows with certainty his initial commodity and money endowment vector $(\bar{x}^{ht}, \bar{m}^{ht})$ where $\bar{m}^{ht}$ is the cash balance carried over from the previous period. An expectation depends on the current price vector π^t and assigns probability to the occurrence of a pair $(\pi^{t+1}, \bar{x}^{ht+1})$ of future price and endowment vectors. This includes market (price) uncertainty and individual (endowment) uncertainty. The von Neumann-Morgenstern utility function u^h is defined on the space of consumption streams over the two periods and m^h gives no direct utility but is used as the only store of value between periods t and $t+1$. It can be shown (see [14]) from the dynamic programming technique discussed above, that the plan x^{ht+1} is a C^{k-1} function $(k > 2)$ of the variables x^{ht}, m^{ht}, and a C^1 function of the parameters π^{t+1} and $\bar{x}^{ht+1}$ for each γ^h in Γ and u^h in U. Hence, the derived expected utility function depends also on money holdings and the current price system. That is,

$$v^h(x^{ht}, m^{ht}, \pi^t; \gamma^h, u^h) = \int u^h(x^{ht}, x^{ht+1}(x^{ht}, m^{ht}; \pi^{t+1}, \bar{x}^{ht+1}))d\gamma^h(\pi^t; \pi^{t+1}, \bar{x}^{ht+1})$$

This also can be viewed as reflecting a generalized real balance effect (see [8]). Note also that $v^h(x^{ht}, m^{ht}, \pi^t; \gamma^h, u^h)$ is in general not homogeneous in money and prices. Thus we allow for the possiblity of money illusion (see [9]). Also, we like to note that v^h is continuously differentiable in all the arguments (including γ^h and u^h) with respect to the "compact-open topology" discussed below. Further, v^h is monotone increasing with respect to x^h and m^h. Finally, if v^h is induced from a utility function u^h which is concave then v^h is also concave with respect to x^h and m^h.

For simplicity we will only work with the differentiable temporary monetary equilibrium framework where there are two periods, for each period there are ℓ commodities and n agents. Also, our analysis is an interior analysis which considers only positive price systems and each agent owns at least a little of each commodity (except money). Since money provides no direct satisfaction, the holding of money could be zero for some agent. The restriction of our analysis to two periods is by no means essential. Although it is assumed that no agent makes plans beyond one period into the future, our analysis carries over to a finitely many period planning horizon.

We are now able to define a space of money economies in period t. First, for each utility function u^h in U and expectation function γ^h in Γ we have an expected utility function v^h defined above. Let P be the commodity space which is the interior of R^{ℓ}_+ and let R_+ be the money space. Thus, at time t, all economic characteristics of the model are completely specified by the product space $(\Gamma \times U \times P \times R_+)^n$ which will be denoted by $\mathscr{E}$, which we will call the space of money economies at time t. It is important to note that in this framework, we allow changes of tastes, changes of beliefs, as well as changes in the commodity endowment and money supply for each agent. We denote a money economy by $E = (\gamma, u, \bar{x}, \bar{m})$ an element of $\mathscr{E}$ where $\gamma = (\gamma^1,\ldots,\gamma^n)$, $u = (u^1,\ldots,u^n)$, $\bar{x} = (\bar{x}^1,\ldots,\bar{x}^n)$, $\bar{m} = (\bar{m}^1,\ldots,\bar{m}^n)$. In other words, E is a list of expectations, utility functions, commodity and money endowments at time t for all agents in the model. Finally, we will also consider the special case of money economies with concave utility functions on the space of consumption streams over two periods denoted by $\mathscr{E}_0$ which is a subspace of $\mathscr{E}$.

We will now discuss the structure of the space of money economies $\mathscr{E}$. First, we note that $\mathscr{E}$ is naturally an infinite dimensional space since utility functions and expectation functions are allowed to vary arbitrarily. Hence, in addition to allowing commodity and money endowments to vary, we also allow tastes and beliefs to vary. This extends Debreu's [4] case (in the general Walrasian equilibrium model) where the space of economies is naturally a finite dimensional Euclidean space since only initial endowments are allowed to vary.[2] The notion of "similarity" of economies can be discussed in terms of the usual Euclidean topology in this latter space which is not sufficient for the case of infinite dimensional spaces where functions are also allowed to vary. Hence, we will need some appropriate topologies to study the notion of "similarity" of infinite dimensional money economies. That is, "similar" money economies must have "similar" characteristics over all the agents. In particular, two "similar" agents must have utility functions, derivatives of the utility functions, expectation functions, derivatives of expectation functions and endowments which are "close" to each other respectively. The notions of "similarity" and "closeness" require the definition of appropriate topologies. Recently, two topologies have been used for infinite dimensional spaces of economies called the compact-open topology [7], [17], [2], [3] and the Whitney topology [17], [14]. The former topology ensures the existence of an equilibrium and the latter topology enables us to study the local characteristics of equilibrium properties such as local uniqueness and stability. From a mathematical viewpoint, two utility functions in U are "close" with respect to the compact-open topology if the functions themselves and their respective derivatives of appropriate order are uniformly "close" on the compact subsets of the

---

[2] In the Walrasian general equilibrium framework, E. and H. Dierker [7] and Smale [17] extended Debreu's [4] case to the cases of allowing demand functions and utility functions to vary respectively.

domain of the utility functions. If the domain is not compact, the notion of "closeness" of utility functions with respect to the Whitney topology is even stronger than uniform "closeness". In other words, the degree of "closeness" is specified by arbitrary positive numbers controlling the "closeness" of the maps and their derivatives respectively. The advantage of using the Whitney topology is that one has as much "control at infinity" as is wanted, and hence there are many important subsets which are open.

To study the properties of local uniqueness and stability of temporary monetary equilibrium it is convenient to define a continuously differentiable map ψ_E from the state space S which is the product space of the commodity space and money space over all agents and the price space to $n(\ell+1) + \ell$ dimensional Euclidean space. The map ψ_E is parameterized by the infinite dimensional space of money economies $\mathcal{E}$ defined above. For every money economy E in $\mathcal{E}$, the map ψ_E specifies the first order conditions for expected utility maximization subject to the budget constraints for every agent and the condition that total demand equals total supply for every commodity and money. An equilibrium state is a point in S such that the map ψ_E takes value zero which is equivalent to saying that all the above equilibrium conditions are satisfied. It is well known that not every equilibrium of an economy varies locally in a continuous and unique manner with the parameters which define the economy. For example, looking into the Edgeworth box for two agents and two commodities, it is easy to construct an economy with a continuum of equilibria. So, a natural question arises. How "large" is the space of economies which satisfies the above equilibrium properties? For the general equilibrium model, this was answered by Debreu in 1970 [4] (see also [6] for a further discussion). In particular, the complement of the space of Arrow-Debreu economies which satisfy the above equilibrium properties is a "negligible" set which, in that finite dimensional framework, means a set of Lebesque measure zero which is also closed [4]. We claim an analogous conclusion for the space of money economies in the temporary equilibrium framework.

In a differentiable framework, the notion of "negligibility" can be defined by a regularity condition on the map ψ_E. We recall that ψ_E is parameterized by the space $\mathcal{E}$, and E in $\mathcal{E}$ is regular if ψ_E has zero as a regular value (see Debreu [6] for a definition of regular value, etc.). Roughly speaking, a money economy is regular if the matrix of derivatives of ψ_E (with respect to x and m) has rank $n(\ell+1)+\ell$ and ψ_E takes value 0 at the point (x,m,π) in S. This is a special case of the general concept of transversality in differential topology [13]. That is, E is regular if ψ_E is transversal to the point zero. Hence, we have available some theorems in transversality theory which can be used on the map ψ_E in our framework (see [14] for a formal application of these theorems to the differentiable temporary equilibrium model). As discussed above, not every economy has determinate equilibrium properties and hence not every map ψ_E is transversal to zero. From Sards' theorem (see Debreu [6] for an excellent discussion) and its various generalizations, transversality is a "generic" quality. That is, any continuous differentiable map f from R^k to R^k no matter how bizarre its behavior with respect to a given point y in R^k, may be deformed by an arbitrarily small amount into a map that is transversal to y. In this sense, almost all maps are transversal to y in R^k. Hence in terms of the map ψ_E, ψ_E is transversal to zero for almost all money economies E in $\mathcal{E}$. In other words, the space of regular money economies denoted by $\mathscr{R}$, a subset of $\mathscr{E}$, is defined by the property that the map ψ_E is transversal to zero and can be shown to be (see [14] for a proof) an "open and dense"[3] subset of $\mathscr{E}$ (where $\mathscr{E}$ is endowed with the Whitney topology). This concept of open-density basically gives a topological expression of largeness. In particular, the space of regular money economies $\mathscr{R}$ is a very large subset of the space of all money economies $\mathscr{E}$ and also, the complement of $\mathscr{R}$ in $\mathscr{E}$ is a closed set with empty interior. In fact the latter is exactly the notion of a "negligible" set from a topological viewpoint discussed above. This means that the set of non-regular money economies in our infinite dimensional space of all money economies is negligible. We like to note that the measure theoretic concept of a negligible set or a closed set of Lebesque measure zero used by Debreu and others is not available for infinite dimensional spaces. Hence, the best we can show at this point is that the set of regular money economies $\mathscr{R}$ is open and dense in the space of all money economies $\mathscr{E}$ and the complement of $\mathscr{R}$ in $\mathscr{E}$ has empty interior. In other words, every money economy in $\mathscr{E}$ can be approximated by a regular money economy in $\mathscr{R}$ and every regular money economy in $\mathscr{R}$ is still regular under small perturbation of the economic characteristics (expectations, utilities and commodity and money endowments) of the model. Since the topological notion of negligibility is weaker than the measure theoretical notion of negligibility, a possible line of further research on this problem might be to introduce a suitable generalization of the concept of Lebesque measure for an infinite dimensional space, and use this measure to study the size of the complement

---

[3] A subset D in a space X is dense in X if the closure of D is equal to X.

of the space $\mathscr{R}$ in $\mathscr{E}$ in addition to the above open-density results.

On the space of regular money economies $\mathscr{R}$, which is open and dense in $\mathscr{E}$, we have shown [14] that this set $\mathscr{R}$ enjoys the desirable properties of locally unique and stable equilibria when $\mathscr{E}$ is endowed with the Whitney topology. That is, almost all money economies have a discrete set of equilibria which varies continuously with respect to the parameters (utilities, expectations and endowments). The local uniqueness property is a consequence of the regularity defined above on the map ψ_E for every E in $\mathscr{R}$ (see [14] for a proof). This property does not require any concavity assumption on the utility functions nor any restrictive assumption such as gross substitutability [1]. The stability or continuity property follows from an application of the implicit function theorem (see [14] for a proof).

Although the set of temporary monetary equilibria is shown to be locally unique and stable for every regular money economy E in $\mathscr{R}$, it is possible that this set is empty. This would be a case of no economic interest. We must also show that this set is nonempty under certain reasonable assumptions in a differentiable framework. Suppose a Debreu type boundary condition is imposed [5], namely that the indifference surfaces do not intersect the boundary of the commodity space. A first implication of this assumption is that the set of temporary monetary equilibria is compact in the state space S (see [14]). Hence, we now have (under this assumption) a stronger version of local uniqueness and stability of temporary monetary equilibrium. That is, for almost all money economies the number of temporary monetary equilibria is finite and they move in a continuous differentiable fashion with respect to changes in the exogeneous economic data of the model. Since the equilibrium set is compact in the state space S, we can now apply some "degree theory" of differential topology [15] to prove the existence of a temporary monetary equilibrium for every money economy in $\mathscr{E}$. Roughly speaking, the degree of a continously differentiable map f from a boundaryless compact set in R^k to R^k is an integer defined by the sum of the "sign" of the derivative matrix of f at x over all x in $f^{-1}(y)$ where y is a regular value of f in R^k. Here the "sign" of the derivative matrix of f at x is +1 or -1 according to whether the determinant of this matrix is positive or negative. It can be shown that the degree of the map f is independent of the choice of the regular value y in R^k. Moreover, the degree is invariant under any continuous deformation of the map f (see [15]). By a suitable modification of the continuously differentiable map ψ_E defined above, one obtains the required conditions for applying degree theory to the model. The basic idea for proving existence of a temporary monetary equilibrium in this differentiable framework, is first to construct a specific regular money economy with concave utility functions which has a unique equilibrium and hence the map ψ_E has degree one. Next, since any two money economies in the space $\mathscr{E}$ can be connected by a continuous path with respect to the compact open topology defined on $\mathscr{E}$, one can perform continuous deformations among money economies including the special case with unique equilibrium. This shows that every money economy has the same degree one and hence every money economy has at least one temporary monetary equilibrium (see [14] for a proof).

Finally, we like to note that the above method of proving existence is in the spirit of counting equations and unknowns, and our whole approach can be considered as a calculus approach to temporary equilibrium theory which originates with the work of Hicks [12]. This approach allows us to obtain the determinate properties (local uniqueness and stability) of temporary equilibrium as well as existence.

References

1. Arrow, K. J. and F. H. Hahn, General Competitive Analysis, Holden-Day, San Francisco, 1971.

2. Chichilnisky, G., and P. J. Kalman, "Special Properties of Critical Points and Operators of Parametrized Manifolds in Economics," Journal of Mathematical Analyses and Applications, Dec. 1976.

3. __________, "Comparative Statics of Less Neoclassical Agents," International Economic Review, forthcoming.

4. Debreu, G., "Economies with a Finite set of Equilibria," Econometrica 38, 1970, pp. 387-392.

5. __________, "Smooth Preferences," Econometrica 40, 1972, pp. 603-615.

6. __________, "Regular Differentiable Economies," American Economic Review, May 1976, pp. 280-287.

7. Dierker, E. and H. Dierker, "On the Local Uniqueness of Equilibria," Econometrica 40, 1972, pp. 867-881.

8. Dusansky, R. and P. J. Kalman, "The Real Balance Effect and the Traditional Theory of Consumer Behavior: A Reconciliation," Journal of Economic Theory 5, 1972, pp. 336-347.

9. __________, "The Foundations of Money Illusion in a Neoclassical Micro-Monetary Model," American Economic Review LXIV, March 1974, pp. 115-122.

10. Grandmont, J.-M., "On the Short-Run Equilibrium in a Monetary Economy," in J. Dreze, ed., Allocation Under Uncertainty: Equilibrium and Optimality, Macmillan, New York, 1974, pp. 213-228.

11. Green, J. R., "Temporary General Equilibrium in a Sequential Trading Model with Spot and Future Transactions," Econometrica 41, 1973, pp. 1103-1124.

12. Hicks, J., Value and Capital, Clarendon Press, 1946.

13. Hirsch, M. W., Notes on Differential Topology, Department of Mathematics, University of California, Berkeley, 1973.

14. Kalman, P. J., and Kuan-Pin Lin, "On Temporary Walrasian Monetary Equilibrium: A Differentiable Approach," Harvard University, July 1976.

15. Milnor, J., Topology from a Differentiable Viewpoint, University of Virginia Press, 1965.

16. Patinkin, D., Money, Interest and Price, Harper and Row, 1965.

17. Smale, S., "Global Analysis and Economics IIA: Extension of a Theorem of Debreu," Journal of Mathematical Economics 1, 1974, pp. 1-14.

18. Smale, S., "Dynamics in General Equilibrium Theory," American Economic Review, May 1976, pp. 288-294.

19. Sondermann, D., "Temporary Competitive Equilibrium Under Uncertainty," in J. Drezè, ed., Allocation Under Uncertainty: Equilibrium and Optimality, Macmillan, New York, 1974, pp. 229-253.

20. Stigum, B. P., "Competitive Equilibria under Uncertainty," Quarterly Journal of Economics 83, 1969, pp. 533-561.

Equilibrium Theory in Veblen-Scitovsky Economies:
Local Uniqueness, Stability and Existence*

by

Peter J. Kalman and Kuan-Pin Lin
and
Hans Wiesmeth

July, 1977

Introduction

The idea that prices influence preferences among commodity vectors goes back to the early works of Veblen [18] and Scitovsky [15]. More recently, Arrow and Hahn [3] formally considered a general equilibrium model for these types of consumers and proved the existence of a general equilibrium. From a comparative static viewpoint, these types of agents have been investigated by Samuelson [14], Kalman [10] and Allingham and Morishima [2], among others.

In this paper we further study these types of agents in a general equilibrium setting using techniques of differential topology recently introduced into the economics literature (see Debreu [5], [6], [7] and Smale [16], [17]). We prove that under certain assumptions, for "almost all" economies there exists a finite number of equilibria (local uniqueness) which are stable. This also implies the existence of equilibrium for all economies. Local

* This work was supported in part by NSF Grant GS 18174. We thank K. J. Arrow, G. Chichilnisky, M. Hirsch, G. Laroque, and J. Wolf for helpful comments. P. J. Kalman is visiting Harvard from SUNY at Stony Brook.

uniqueness is obtained without requiring any convexity assumptions on preferences. This paper can be considered as an extension of Arrow and Hahn's work in [3] to the study of the structure of the set of equilibria. We study utility functions directly and do not require well defined demand functions. However, our class of utility functions includes those which define continuously differentiable demand functions. We do not need homogeneity assumptions on price-influenced utility functions or induced demand functions.[1] In general, demand functions may exhibit money illusion in this model.

II. The Model

We consider a space of economies with price influenced utilities, ℓ commodities and n agents. Let R^{ℓ}_{+} be the commodity space[2] where for each agent h, $(h = 1, \ldots, n)$, $x^h \in R^{\ell}_{+}$ is the consumption of agent h. Suppose $S = \{p \in R^{\ell}_{+}: \Sigma^{\ell}_{i=1} p_i = 1\}$ is the price space. Let $\bar{x}^h$ denote the resource endowment of agent h, and his utility function is a real-valued function defined by $u^h: R^{\ell}_{+} \times S \to R$. We assume that $\bar{x}^h$ is strictly positive and $u^h(\cdot, p)$ is twice continuously differentiable with respect to x^h for each $p \in S$. Further, we assume u^h is continuously differentiable in all arguments and that $u^h(\cdot, p)$ fulfills a technical boundary condition (for instance, see Smale [16]) and it satisfies a monotonicity hypothesis for any $p \in S$. In summary, we make the following assumptions for each agent h:

---

[1] That is, utility functions do not have to be homogeneous of any degree in prices and demand functions do not have to be homogeneous of degree zero in prices and wealth, see [2] and [10].

[2] This R^{ℓ}_{+} is not a manifold nor a manifold with boundary. However a submanifold of R^{ℓ}_{+} can be defined as follows: Let U be an open set of R^{ℓ}_{+}, then a submanifold of R^{ℓ}_{+} is a subset of R^{ℓ}_{+} of the form $V \cap R^{\ell}_{+}$ where V is a submanifold of U.

A. 1 $\bar{x}^h \in \mathring{R}^\ell_+$,

A. 2 $u^h \in C^1(R^\ell_+ \times S, R)$ and $u^h(\cdot, p) \in C^2(R^\ell_+, R)$ for each $p \in S$.

A. 3 (Boundary Condition) For any $p \in S$, if $x^h \in \partial R^\ell_+$, $D_1 u^h(x^h, p) \cdot (\bar{x}^h - x^h) > 0$

and

A. 4 (Monotonicity) $D_1 u^h(x^h, p) \in \mathring{R}^\ell_+$,

where $\mathring{R}^\ell_+$ denotes the interior of R^ℓ_+, and $\partial R^\ell_+ = R^\ell_+ - \mathring{R}^\ell_+$ is the boundary. $C^1(R^\ell_+ \times S, R)$ and $C^2(R^\ell_+, R)$ denote the spaces of once and twice continuously differentiable functions from $R^\ell_+ \times S$ to R and R^ℓ_+ to R respectively. $D_1 u^h(x^h, p)$ is the derivative of u^h with respect to the coordinates of x^h. Loosely speaking, A. 3 restricts the behavior of the indifference surfaces at the boundary of the commodity space, and A. 4 states that every commodity is desired by every agent independent of the price system. A. 1 is assumed so that A. 3 and A. 4 can be compatible. We could weaken A. 1 by replacing it by $\bar{x}^h \in R^\ell_+ - \{0\}$ without changing our results. Although A. 1, A. 3 and A. 4 are unnecessarily strong for the "generic" results of Section III, we assume that these assumptions hold throughout the paper. Let $\mathcal{U}(R^\ell_+ \times S, R) = \{u^h \in C^1(R^\ell_+ \times S, R): $ A. 2, A. 3 and A. 4 are satisfied$\}$. $\mathcal{U}$ is called the space of utility functions for every agent h. For a special case of $\mathcal{U}$, we shall also consider a subspace of utility functions which possess a convexity property, i. e., $\mathcal{U}_0(R^\ell_+ \times S, R) = \{u^h \in \mathcal{U}(R^\ell_+ \times S, R): D_1^2 u^h(x^h, p)|_{\ker D_1 u^h(x^h, p)}$ is negative definite for each $(x^h, p) \in R^\ell_+ \times S\}$. Since the total endowment as well as its distribution are also allowed to vary in $\mathring{R}^\ell_+$, the economic characteristics of our model are completely specified by the product space $(\mathcal{U} \times \mathring{R}^\ell_+)^n$ denoted by $\mathcal{E}$ and $E = (u, \bar{x}) \in \mathcal{E}$ where $u = (u^1, \ldots, u^n)$ and $\bar{x} = (\bar{x}^1, \ldots, \bar{x}^n)$. Then, an economy E is a list of price influenced utility functions and resource endowments, and $\mathscr{E}$ is called the space of economies. In particular, $\mathscr{E}_0 = (\mathscr{U}_0 \times \mathring{R}^{\ell}_{+})^n$ is the space of convex economies. On the space $\mathscr{E}$, we shall consider two different topologies for different purposes, called "strong" and "weak" topologies, respectively. For dealing with "generic" properties, as we do in Section III, the most useful topology on $\mathscr{E}$ is the strong topology defined by the product of the induced Whitney C^1 topology on $\mathscr{U}^n$ and the induced usual topology on $\mathring{R}^{\ell n}_{+}$, provided $C^2(R^{\ell}_{+}, R)$ is endowed with the Whitney C^2 topology. It is an extremely large topology which controls the closeness of the maps and their derivatives. Although the strong topology defined on $\mathscr{E}$ is very convenient in that many important subsets are open, the space $\mathscr{E}$ is not metrizable and in fact does not have a countable base at any point. Because of these latter inconvenient properties, the weak topology on $\mathscr{E}$ is defined by replacing the Whitney C^1 topology and Whitney C^2 topology by the C^1 compact-open topology and C^2 compact-open topology on $C^1(R^{\ell}_{+} \times S, R)$ and $C^2(R^{\ell}_{+}, R)$, respectively.[3] This weak topology is used for proving existence.

As usual, for every price influenced economy $E = (u, \bar{x}) \in \mathscr{E}$, the wealth of agent h at a prevailing price system $p \in S$ denoted y^h is defined by the inner product of p and $\bar{x}^h$, i.e. $y^h(p, \bar{x}^h) = p \cdot \bar{x}^h$, and the budget set $B^h(p, y^h) = \{x^h \in R^{\ell}_{+} : p \cdot x^h = y^h\}$. Given a C^1 utility function $u^h : R^{\ell}_{+} \times S \to R$ with $u^h(\cdot, p) \in C^2(R^{\ell}_{+}, R)$, the induced demand functions may not be well defined (see Katzner [11] for an example). However, C^1 demand functions are globally defined in the space of convex economies, $\mathscr{E}_0$. For every economy $E \in \mathscr{E}$, an equilibrium is an allocation-price pair (x, p) with

---

[3] For a definition of Whitney C^k topology and C^k compact-open topology on $C^k(X, Y)$, see Hirsch [9] and Smale [16].

$$\sum_{h=1}^{n} x^h = \sum_{h=1}^{n} \bar{x}^h ,$$

and x^h is a maximal point of $u^h(\cdot, p)$ restricted to the budget set $B^h(p, y^h)$ for every h. We recall that if $f:X \to Y$ is class C^1, a point $x \in X$ is a regular point of f if $Df(x):T_xX \to T_yY$ is surjective with $y = f(x)$ where $Df(x)$ represents the derivative of the map f computed at x, which is a linear map from the tangent space of X at x to the tangent space of Y at y, denoted by T_xX and T_yY, respectively. If $Df(x)$ is not surjective, x is a critical point of f. y is called a regular value if every $x \in f^{-1}(y)$ is a regular point. y is a critical value if at least one $x \in f^{-1}(y)$ is a critical point. For $p \in S$, the condition for x^h to be a critical point of $u^h(x^h, p)$ restricted to $B^h(p, y^h)$ can be written as $D_1u^h(x^h, p) = \lambda^h p$ where λ^h is the Lagrangian multiplier. To avoid λ^h in the model, we substitute

$$\lambda^h = |D_1u^h(x^h, p)|$$

where

$$|D_1u^h(x^h, p)| = \sum_{i=1}^{\ell} \frac{\partial u^h}{\partial x_i^h} (x^h, p) .$$

It is obvious that $\lambda^h > 0$ for every h by A. 4. We formally define the set of <u>equilibria</u> for $E \in \mathcal{E}$ as

$$W(E) = \left\{ (x, p) \in R_+^{\ell n} \times S : u^h(x^h, p) \text{ is maximized, } px^h = p\bar{x}^h,\ h = 1, \ldots, n, \text{ and } \sum_{h=1}^{n} x^h = \sum_{h=1}^{n} \bar{x}^h \right\} ,$$

and the set of <u>extended equilibria</u> for $E \in \mathcal{E}$ as

$$\Phi(E) = \left\{ (x, p) \in R_+^{\ell n} \times S: D_1 u^h(x^h, p) = |D_1 u^h(x^h, p)| \cdot p , \right.$$

$$\left. px^h = p\bar{x}^h,\ h = 1, \ldots, n, \text{ and } \sum_{h=1}^{n} x^h = \sum_{h=1}^{n} \bar{x}^h \right\} .$$

The concept of extended equilibria for the classical model in which u^h is independent of the price system was first used by Smale [16]. Since the condition $px^n = p\bar{x}^n$ can be obtained from $px^h = p\bar{x}^h$, $h = 1, \ldots, n-1$, and

$$\sum_{h=1}^{n} x^h = \sum_{h=1}^{n} \bar{x}^h ,$$

the set of extended equilibria for every $E \in \mathscr{E}$ can be rewritten as

$$\Phi(E) = \left\{ (x, p) \in R_+^{\ell n} \times S: D_1 u^h(x^h, p) = |D_1 u^h(x^h, p)| \cdot p ,\ h = 1, \ldots, n , \right.$$

$$\left. px^h = p\bar{x}^h,\ h = 1, \ldots, n-1, \text{ and } \sum_{h=1}^{n} x^h = \sum_{h=1}^{n} \bar{x}^h \right\} .$$

For every economy $E = (u, \bar{x}) \in \mathscr{E}$, we define a map $\psi_E: R_+^{\ell n} \times S \to I^n \times R^{n+\ell-1}$ by

$$\psi_E(x, p) = \Big(D_1 u^h(x^h, p) - |D_1 u^h(x^h, p)| \cdot p,\ h = 1, \ldots, n;\ p\bar{x}^h - px^h,\ h = 1, \ldots, n-1$$

$$\sum_{h=1}^{n} \bar{x}^h - \sum_{h=1}^{n} x^h \Big)$$

where $I = \{ z \in R^\ell : \Sigma_{i=1}^{\ell} z_i = 0 \} \subset R^\ell$. Obviously, $\psi_E \in C^1(R_+^{\ell n} \times S, I^n \times R^{n+\ell-1})$ since for every h, $u^h \in C^1(R_+^\ell \times S, R)$ and $u^h(\cdot, p) \in C^2(R_+^\ell, R)$ for every $p \in S$. By definition of $\Phi(E)$, we have $\Phi(E) = \psi_E^{-1}(0)$, and $W(E) \subset \Phi(E)$ for every $E \in \mathscr{E}$. The latter follows from A. 3 and the Kuhn-Tucker Theorem. That is, if (x, p) is an equilibrium, it is an extended equilibrium, and the C^1 map ψ_E vanishes at (x, p). It is clear that $W(E) = \psi_E^{-1}(0)$ for every convex, price influenced economy, i.e., $\forall E \in \mathscr{E}_0$. If $(x, p) \in \Phi(E)$ for an economy $E \in \mathscr{E}$, we get $D_1 u^h(x^h, p)(\bar{x}^h - x^h) = 0$ for every agent h. From A. 3 and A. 4, $(x, p) \notin \partial(R_+^{\ell n} \times S)$ for every $(x, p) \in \Phi(E)$. Next, if there is a sequence $\{(x^q, p^q)\}$ with $(x^q, p^q) \in \Phi(E)$ for every q such that (x^q, p^q) converges to (x^0, p^0), then $(x^0, p^0) \in \Phi(E)$ since $\Phi(E) = \psi_E^{-1}(0)$ and ψ_E is C^1. Thus $\Phi(E)$ is closed. Hence, we have the following

PROPOSITION 1. $\Phi(E)$ is compact-valued for every $E \in \mathscr{E}$, and $\Phi(E) \subset \mathring{R}_+^{\ell n} \times \mathring{S}$.

III. Local Uniqueness and Stability of Equilibria

In this section we prove local uniqueness and stability of extended (and classical) equilibria for ''almost all'' economies in $\mathscr{E}$ which is defined by a regularity condition on ψ_E below.[4] We first recall a concept of transversality in differential topology. Let Z be a submanifold of Y, $f \in C^1(X, Y)$ is said to be transversal to Z at $x \in X$, denoted by $f \pitchfork_x Z$, if either $y = f(x) \notin Z$ or $y = f(x) \in Z$ and $Df(x)[T_x X] + T_y Z = T_y Y$, i.e., the image of $Df(x)$ and $T_y Z$ as subspaces of $T_y Y$ span $T_y Y$. If $f \pitchfork_x Z$ for every $x \in X$, $f \pitchfork Z$. From Sard's theorem, transversality is a generic quality. In this sense, almost all mappings are transversal. In view of the space of economies, the notion of

[4] As in [16] and [17], the local uniqueness and stability of equilibria can be obtained under weaker conditions, that is, there is no need to assume $\bar{x}^h \in \mathring{R}_+^\ell$, nor any boundary conditions nor monotonicity on u^h for each h in the model.

transversality makes sense in the model. We claim that the subspace of economies satisfying a transversality requirement is open and dense. Actually, we apply the concept of transversality only in the very special sense of the above consideration. That is, Z is just a single point y, and therefore its tangent space is the zero subspace of $T_y Y$. Thus, f is transversal to y if either $y \neq f(x)$ for all x or $Df(x)[T_x X] = T_y Y$ for all $x \in f^{-1}(y)$, which is to say that y is a regular value of f. So transversality includes the notion of regularity as a special case. In fact, f is regular if and only if $f \pitchfork y$ for every $y \in Y$. Now, we need a few definitions. An element $E \in \mathscr{E}$ is called a <u>regular economy</u> if and only if the associated map ψ_E is transversal to the origin, i.e., $\psi_E \pitchfork 0$. Moreover, the space of regular economies is denoted by the set $\mathscr{R} = \{E \in \mathscr{E}\colon \psi_E \pitchfork 0\}$ and the space of convex regular economies is $\mathscr{R}_0 = \mathscr{R} \cap \mathscr{E}_0$. By a theorem of differential topology (for instance see [1], p. 45), $\psi_E^{-1}(0) = \Phi(E)$ is a C^1 submanifold of $R_+^{\ell n} \times S$ for every $E \in \mathscr{R}$.

PROPOSITION 2. <u>$\mathscr{R}$ is open and dense in $\mathscr{E}$ with respect to the strong topology.</u>[5]

<u>Proof</u>: Since R_+^ℓ is locally compact, we let $\{K_\alpha\}$ be a sequence of compact sets in R_+^ℓ with $K_\alpha \subset K_{\alpha+1}$ and $R_+^\ell = \cup_\alpha K_\alpha$. For $u^h \in C^1(R_+^\ell \times S, R)$, let $u_\alpha^h = u^h | K_\alpha \times S \in C^1(K_\alpha \times S, R)$ for each α.

---

[5] The density and openness of $\mathscr{R}$ in $\mathscr{E}$ implies that any economy can be approximated by a regular economy and any regular economy is still regular under small perturbation of economic data in the model.

The spaces $C^1(K_\alpha \times S, R)$ are Banach spaces (see [1], p. 24). Moreover, they are metrizable and separable, hence they are second countable (see [12]). Furthermore, the space $C^1(R_+^\ell \times S, R)$ is the inverse limit[6] of the sequence $\{C^1(K_\alpha \times S, R), f_\alpha\}$. That is $f_\alpha : C^1(K_\alpha \times S, R) \to C^1(K_{\alpha-1} \times S, R)$ defined by $f_\alpha(u_\alpha^h) = u_{\alpha-1}^h = u_\alpha^h | K_{\alpha-1} \times S$ is clearly continuous. Define

$$\mathcal{U}_\alpha = \{u_\alpha^h \in C^1(K_\alpha \times S, R) : \text{A.2, A.3 and A.4 are satisfied}\}$$

and $\mathcal{E}_\alpha = (\mathcal{U}_\alpha \times \overset{\circ}{R}{}_+^\ell)^n$, then $\mathcal{U}$ and $\mathcal{E}$ are the inverse limit spaces of $\{\mathcal{U}_\alpha, f'_\alpha\}$ and $\{\mathcal{E}_\alpha, g_\alpha\}$ respectively, where $f'_\alpha = f_\alpha | \mathcal{U}_\alpha$, $g_\alpha : \mathcal{E}_\alpha \to \mathcal{E}_{\alpha-1}$ defined by

$$g_\alpha = (\underbrace{f'_\alpha, \cdots, f'_\alpha}_{n \text{ times}}, \text{ id})$$

and id, the identity map, from $\overset{\circ}{R}{}_+^{\ell n}$ to $\overset{\circ}{R}{}_+^{\ell n}$. Clearly, $\mathcal{E}_\alpha$ is a C^1 (Banach) manifold and second countable. Define the sequence $\{\mathcal{R}_\alpha, g'_\alpha\}$ as $\mathcal{R}_\alpha = \{E_\alpha \in \mathcal{E}_\alpha : \psi_{E_\alpha} \pitchfork 0\}$, $g'_\alpha = g_\alpha | \mathcal{R}_\alpha$ and $\psi_{E_\alpha} = \psi_E | K_\alpha^n \times S$. Then $\mathcal{R}$ is the inverse limit of $\{\mathcal{R}_\alpha, g'_\alpha\}$. We claim that $\mathcal{R}_\alpha$ is open and dense in $\mathcal{E}_\alpha$ for each α. We apply the transversal density theorem 19.1 of [1], p. 48. Conditions (1), (2) and (3) of 19.1 are satisfied. We need to check condition (4) of Theorem 19.1 of [1]. First, let $\psi_\alpha : \mathcal{E}_\alpha \times K_\alpha^n \times S \to I^n \times R^{n+\ell-1}$ defined by $\psi_\alpha(E_\alpha, x, p) = \psi_{E_\alpha}(x, p)$ for each $E_\alpha \in \mathcal{E}_\alpha$ and $(x, p) \in K_\alpha^n \times S$ be the evaluation map of ψ_{E_α}. It is clear that ψ_α is C^1 (for instance, see [1], p. 25). We go on to prove that the evaluation map ψ_α is transversal to 0, i.e., $\psi_\alpha \pitchfork 0$. By definition, $\psi_\alpha : \mathcal{E}_\alpha \times K_\alpha^n \times S \to I^n \times R^{n+\ell-1}$ is given by

---

[6] Let X_α be a topological space and f_α be a continuous map from X_α into $X_{\alpha-1}$, for each α. The sequence $\{X_\alpha, f_\alpha\}$ is called an inverse limit sequence. The inverse limit space of the sequence $\{X_\alpha, f_\alpha\}$ is the following subset of $\Pi_\alpha X_\alpha : X = \{x \in \Pi_\alpha X_\alpha : f_\alpha(x_\alpha) = x_{\alpha-1}$ for each α and $x_\alpha \in X_\alpha$, $x_{\alpha-1} \in X_{\alpha-1}\}$ (see [19], p. 217).

$$\psi_\alpha(E_\alpha, x, p) = \left(D_1 u_\alpha^h(x^h, p) - |D_1 u_\alpha^h(x^h, p)| \cdot p, \ h = 1, \ldots, n; \ p\overline{x}^h - px^h, \right.$$

$$h = 1, \ldots, n-1;$$

$$\left. \sum_{h=1}^n \overline{x}^h - \sum_{h=1}^n x^h \right)$$

Its derivative

$$D\psi_\alpha(E_\alpha, x, p) : T_{(E_\alpha, x, p)}(\mathscr{E}_\alpha \times K_\alpha^n \times S) \rightarrow T_{\psi_\alpha(E_\alpha, x, p)}(I^n \times R^{n+\ell-1})$$

at (E_α, x, p) is defined by

$$D\psi_\alpha(E_\alpha, x, p)(\dot{E}_\alpha, \dot{x}, \dot{p})$$

$$= \left(\frac{\partial^2 u_\alpha^h}{\partial x_k^h \partial E_\alpha} \dot{E}_\alpha - \sum_{i=1}^\ell \frac{\partial^2 u_\alpha^h}{\partial x_i^h \partial E_\alpha} p_k \dot{E}_\alpha + \sum_{j=1}^\ell \frac{\partial^2 u_\alpha^h}{\partial x_k^h \partial x_j^h} \dot{x}_j^h - \sum_{j=1}^\ell \sum_{i=1}^\ell \frac{\partial^2 u_\alpha^h}{\partial x_i^h \partial x_j^h} p_k \dot{x}_j^h \right.$$

$$+ \sum_{j=1}^\ell \frac{\partial^2 u_\alpha^h}{\partial x_k^h \partial p_j} \dot{p}_j - \sum_{j=1}^\ell \sum_{i=1}^\ell \frac{\partial^2 u_\alpha^h}{\partial x_i^h \partial p_j} p_k \dot{p}_j - \sum_{i=1}^\ell \frac{\partial u_\alpha^h}{\partial x_i^h} \dot{p}_k \ ,$$

$$k = 1, \ldots, \ell \ ,$$
$$h = 1, \ldots, n \ ,$$

$$\left. \dot{p}(\overline{x}^h - x^h) + p(\dot{\overline{x}}^h - \dot{x}^h) \ , \ h = 1, \ldots, n-1, \ \sum_{h=1}^n \dot{\overline{x}}^h - \sum_{h=1}^n \dot{x}^h \right) \ ,$$

where $(\dot{E}_\alpha, \dot{x}, \dot{p}) \in T_{(E_\alpha, x, p)}(\mathscr{E}_\alpha \times K_\alpha^n \times S)$ and $\dot{E}_\alpha = (\dot{u}_\alpha, \dot{\overline{x}})$. Without loss of generality, we take $\dot{E}_\alpha = (0, \dot{\overline{x}})$ and $\dot{x} = 0$. Then

$D\psi_a(E_a, x, p)((0, \dot{\bar{x}}), 0, \dot{p})$

$$= \left(\sum_{j=1}^{\ell} \frac{\partial^2 u_a^h}{\partial x_k^h \partial p_j} \dot{p}_j - \sum_{j=1}^{\ell} \sum_{i=1}^{\ell} \frac{\partial^2 u_a^h}{\partial x_i^h \partial p_j} p_k p_j - \sum_{i=1}^{\ell} \frac{\partial u_a^h}{\partial x_i^h} \dot{p}_k, \quad k = 1, \ldots, \ell, \quad h = 1, \ldots, n, \right.$$

$$\left. \dot{p} \cdot (\bar{x}^h - x^h) + p \cdot \dot{\bar{x}}^h, \quad h = 1, \ldots, n-1, \quad \sum_{h=1}^{n} \dot{\bar{x}}^h \right) .$$

For each $(a, b, c) \in T_{\psi_a(E_a, x, p)}(I^n \times R^{n+\ell-1})$ with $a = (a^1, \ldots, a^n) \in T_{\psi_a(E_a, x, p)}(I^n)$, $b = (b^1, \ldots, b^{n-1}) \in R^{n-1}$ and $c = (c_1, \ldots, c_\ell) \in R^\ell$, there exists

$$((0, \dot{\bar{x}}), 0, \dot{p}) \in T_{(E_a, x, p)}(\mathscr{E}_a \times K_a^n \times S)$$

such that $D\psi_a(E_a, x, p)((0, \dot{\bar{x}}), 0, \dot{p}) = (a, b, c)$ since

$$\sum_{k=1}^{\ell} a_k^h = 0 , \qquad \sum_{i=1}^{\ell} \frac{\partial u_a^h}{\partial x_i^h} > 0$$

for each h and $p \neq 0$. Therefore, $D\psi_a(E_a, x, p)$ is surjective on

$$T_{\psi_a(E_a, x, p)}(I^n \times R^{n+\ell-1}) .$$

In particular, $\psi_a \pitchfork 0$. This shows that condition (4) of the transversal density theorem 19.1 of [1] is satisfied. Hence $\mathscr{R}_a$ is dense in $\mathscr{E}_a$. The openness of $\mathscr{R}_a$ in $\mathscr{E}_a$ follows from the openness of transversal intersection theorem 18.2 of [1], p. 47.

Let $r_a : \mathscr{E} \to \mathscr{E}_a$ for every a be the canonical restriction maps. To prove that $\mathscr{R}$ is open and dense in $\mathscr{E}$ with respect to the strong topology, we first claim that $r_a^{-1}(\mathscr{R}_a)$ is dense in $\mathscr{E}$ with respect to the strong topology. We note that r_a is not an open map with respect to the strong topology on $\mathscr{E}$. But in fact, we do not need the openness of r_a, and it would suffice if we know that the image of an open set of $\mathscr{E}$ under r_a contains an open set of $\mathscr{E}_a$. Let $N(E) = N^{\epsilon}(u) \times N(\bar{x})$ be a neighborhood of $E = (u, \bar{x})$ in $\mathscr{E}$ with respect to the strong topology, where $N(\bar{x})$ is an usual neighborhood of $\bar{x}$ in $\overset{\circ}{R}{}^{\ell}_{+}$ and $N^{\epsilon}(u) = \{u' \in \mathscr{U}^n : \| D^k u^h(x^h, p) - D^k u^{h'}(x^h, p) \| < \epsilon^h(x^h, p)$ for all $(x^h, p) \in R^{\ell}_{+} \times S$, $k = 0, 1$ and $h = 1, \ldots, n\}$ with $\epsilon^h : R^{\ell}_{+} \times S \to R$ being a positive continuous function for each h. As we discuss earlier, $r_a(N(E)) \subset \mathscr{E}_a$ is not an open set in general. However, if we shrink $N(E)$ to a neighborhood $N^*(E) = N^{\delta}(u) \times N(\bar{x})$ with $\delta^h \leq \epsilon^h$ and $\delta^h : R^{\ell}_{+} \times S \to R$ is a positive continuous function and increasing with respect to $x^h \in R^{\ell}_{+}$ for every h, it is obvious that for every $E'_a = (u'_a, \bar{x}') \in N^*_a(E_a) = N^{\delta}_a(u_a) \times N(\bar{x})$, $u^{h'}_a$ can be extended to a function $u^{h'} \in \mathscr{U}$ with $u^{h'}_a = u^{h'} | K_a \times S$ for every h, where $N^{\delta}_a(u_a) = \{u'_a \in \mathscr{U}^n_a : \| D^k u^h_a(x^h, p) - D^k u^{h'}_a(x^h, p) \| < \delta^h(x^h, p)$ for every $(x^h, p) \in K_a \times S$, $k = 0, 1$, and $h = 1, \ldots, n\}$. Hence $r_a(N^*(E)) = N^*_a(E_a)$ is open in $\mathscr{E}_a$ and consequently $r_a(N(E))$ contains an open set. Together with the fact that $\mathscr{R}_a$ is dense in $\mathscr{E}_a$, we have $r_a(N(E)) \cap \mathscr{R}_a \neq \phi$. This means that there exists an $E' \in N(E)$ such that $r_a(E') \in \mathscr{R}_a$ or $E' \in r_a^{-1}(\mathscr{R}_a)$. Hence $N(E) \cap r_a^{-1}(\mathscr{R}_a) \neq \phi$, or equivalently $r_a^{-1}(\mathscr{R}_a)$ is dense in $\mathscr{E}$. By definition, $\mathscr{R} = \cap_a r_a^{-1}(\mathscr{R}_a)$. Therefore, $\mathscr{R}$ is dense in $\mathscr{E}$ with respect to the strong topology since $\mathscr{E}$ is a Baire space. Moreover, if $E \in \mathscr{R}$, then by definition, $E_a \in \mathscr{R}_a$ with $g'_a(E_a) = E_{a-1}$ for each a. Since $\mathscr{R}_a$ is open in $\mathscr{E}_a$, there exists a neighborhood $N_a(E_a) = N^{\epsilon}_a(u_a) \times N(\bar{x})$ of E_a in $\mathscr{E}_a$ with $N_a(E_a) \subset \mathscr{R}_a$ for each α. In particular, $N^{\varepsilon}_{\alpha}(u_{\alpha}) = \{u'_{\alpha} \in \mathscr{U}^{n}_{\alpha} : \| D^{k}u^{h}_{\alpha}(x^{h}, p) - D^{k}u^{h'}_{\alpha}(x^{h}, p)\| < \varepsilon^{h}_{\alpha}(x^{h}, p)$ for every $(x^{h}, p) \in K_{\alpha} \times S$, $k = 0, 1$ and $h = 1, \ldots, n\}$, where $\varepsilon^{h}_{\alpha} : K_{\alpha} \times S \to R$ is a positive continuous function for every h. We now choose a positive continuous function $\delta^{h} : R^{\ell}_{+} \times S \to R$ with $\delta^{h}(x^{h}, p) \le \varepsilon^{h}_{\alpha}(x^{h}, p)$ for every $(x^{h}, p) \in K_{\alpha} \times S$ and all α. Then $N^{*}(E) = N^{\delta}(u) \times N(\bar{x})$ is a neighborhood of E in $\mathscr{E}$ and $N^{*}(E) \subset \mathscr{R}$. Hence the openness of $\mathscr{R}$ in $\mathscr{E}$ follows. Q. E. D.

We now prove the stability theorem.

THEOREM 1. The extended equilibrium correspondence $\Phi : \mathscr{R} \to R^{\ell n}_{+} \times S$ defined by $\Phi(E) = \psi^{-1}_{E}(0)$ for every $E \in \mathscr{R}$ is continuous, i. e., Φ is stable for every $E \in \mathscr{R}$, with respect to the strong topology.

Proof. For every regular economy $E \in \mathscr{R}$, we have $\psi_{E} \pitchfork 0$. By the openness property of $\mathscr{R}$, $\psi_{E'} \pitchfork 0$ for $E' \in \mathscr{R}$ near E. We claim that for E' near E, $\psi^{-1}_{E'}(0)$ and $\psi^{-1}_{E}(0)$ are close to each other, i. e., the extended equilibrium correspondence $\Phi : \mathscr{R} \to R^{\ell n}_{+} \times S$ is continuous. In fact, $\psi_{\alpha} : \mathscr{E}_{\alpha} \times K^{n}_{\alpha} \times S \to I^{n} \times R^{n+\ell-1}$ is C^{1}. Moreover, for every $E_{\alpha} \in \mathscr{R}_{\alpha}$, $\psi_{E_{\alpha}}$ is a C^{1} local diffeomorphism by the inverse function theorem since $D\psi_{E_{\alpha}}(x, p) : T_{(x,p)}(K^{n}_{\alpha} \times S) \to T_{\psi_{E_{\alpha}}(x,p)}(I^{n} \times R^{n+\ell-1})$ with $(x, p) \in \psi^{-1}_{E_{\alpha}}(0)$, is an isomorphism. Hence, the stability property of the map $\Phi_{\alpha} = \Phi | \mathscr{R}_{\alpha} : \mathscr{R}_{\alpha} \to R^{\ell n}_{+} \times S$ follows by an application of the implicit function theorem on the evaluation map ψ_{α}. That is, there exist neighborhoods $N_{\alpha}(E_{\alpha})$ of $E_{\alpha} \in \mathscr{R}_{\alpha}$ and V of $(x, p) \in K^{n}_{\alpha} \times S \subset R^{\ell n}_{+} \times S$, and a C^{1} function $\xi_{\alpha} : N_{\alpha}(E_{\alpha}) \to V$ such that $\psi_{\alpha}(E'_{\alpha}, \xi_{\alpha}(E'_{\alpha})) = 0$ for every $E'_{\alpha} \in N_{\alpha}(E_{\alpha})$ and $\xi_{\alpha}(E_{\alpha}) = (x, p)$. Since $\Phi_{\alpha-1}(E_{\alpha-1}) \subset \Phi_{\alpha}(E_{\alpha})$ for every α, we have the following diagram

$$\begin{array}{ccc} N_{a-1}(E_{a-1}) & \xleftarrow{\;g'_a | N_a(E_a)\;} & N_a(E_a) \\ \downarrow \xi_{a-1} & & \downarrow \xi_a \\ V & \xleftarrow{\;id\;} & V \end{array}$$

which is commutative, i.e., $\xi_{a-1} \circ g'_a | N_a(E_a) = id \circ \xi_a$ for every a. This implies that at the inverse limit there is a continuous function $\xi : N^*(E) \to V$ such that $\psi(E', \xi(E')) = 0$ for every $E' \in N^*(E)$ and $\xi(E) = (x, p)$, where $N^*(E)$ is a neighborhood as constructed in the proof of Proposition 2. Hence the extended equilibrium correspondence Φ is stable for every $E \in \mathscr{R}$ with respect to the strong topology. Q. E. D.

COROLLARY 1. The equilibrium correspondence defined on the space of convex regular economies is continuous, i. e., $W : \mathscr{R}_0 \to R_+^{\ell n} \times S$ is stable, with respect to the strong topology.

Next we prove local uniqueness of the equilibria for an open and dense subset $\mathscr{R}$ of the space of all economies $\mathscr{E}$ with respect to the strong topology.

THEOREM 2. For every regular economy $E = (u, \bar{x}) \in \mathscr{R}$, the extended equilibrium set $\Phi(E)$ is a finite set.

Proof. Since $\Phi(E) = \psi_E^{-1}(0)$ is compact for every $E \in \mathscr{E}$ by Proposition 1, and $\psi_E^{-1}(0)$ is a submanifold with zero dimension if $E \in \mathscr{R}$, $\Phi(E)$ is a finite set. Q. E. D.

COROLLARY 2. For every regular economy $E \in \mathscr{R}$, the equilibrium set $W(E)$ is also a finite set.

IV. Existence of Equilibrium

Although the number of extended (or classical) equilibria for every regular economy E is finite, it is possible that $\Phi(E)$ or $W(E)$ is an empty set. To show $\Phi(E) \neq \phi$ and $W(E) \neq \phi$ we first prove the following:

PROPOSITION 3. There exists a regular convex economy with unique extended equilibrium.

Proof. We prove this proposition by considering a nonempty subset of $\mathscr{U}_0$ for each agent, which contains additive separable utility functions with respect to x^h and p, denoted by $\mathscr{U}_{S0} \subset \mathscr{U}_0 \subset \mathscr{U}$. Define $\mathscr{E}_{S0} = (\mathscr{U}_{S0} \times \mathring{R}^{\ell}_{+})^n$, then $\mathscr{E}_{S0} \subset \mathscr{E}_0 \subset \mathscr{E}$. For an $E = (u, \bar{x}) \in \mathscr{E}_{S0}$, let $\bar{x}$ be an equilibrium allocation (this is possible if we choose $E = (u, \bar{x})$ with $u^1 = \cdots = u^n$, $\bar{x}^1 = \cdots = \bar{x}^n$). Then, by continuous differentiability and monotonicity of u^h for every h, there exists a unique $p^* \in S$ such that $\psi_E(\bar{x}, p^*) = 0$. In particular,

$$D_1 u^h(\bar{x}^h, p^*) = |D_1 u^h(\bar{x}^h, p^*)| \cdot p^*$$

for every agent h. Since $u^h \in \mathscr{U}_0$, by a well-known result of consumer theory on convex preferences (for instance, see [14]), $p^* x^h > p^* \bar{x}^h$ for every h with $x^h \neq \bar{x}^h$ and $\psi_E(x, p^*) = 0$. This is a self-contradiction. Hence $(\bar{x}, p^*)$ is a unique equilibrium for E. Furthermore, we need to check that the matrix $D\psi_E$ has rank

$\ell n + \ell - 1$ at $(\bar{x}, p^*)$. This follows from the fact that for each agent h, $|D_1 u^h(\bar{x}^h, p^*)| > 0$ and $D_1^2 u^h(\bar{x}^h, p^*)$ as a bilinear symmetric form on the space $\ker D_1 u^h(\bar{x}^h, p^*) = \{v \in R^{\ell n}: D_1 u^h(\bar{x}^h, p^*)(v) = 0\}$ is negative definite. Hence $E = (u, \bar{x}) \in \mathscr{R}$. Q. E. D.

As a matter of fact, the strong topology defined on $\mathscr{E}$, which establishes the generic local uniqueness and stability of equilibrium, does not make the space $\mathscr{E}$ a topological vector space since $R_+^{\ell n} \times S$ is certainly noncompact. Toward proving the existence theorem, we need the weak topology on $\mathscr{E}$. It is obvious that the weak topology on $\mathscr{E}$ does not control the behavior of the maps and their derivatives "at infinity" very well, but it would make $\mathscr{E}$ metrizable. We now prove an existence theorem.

THEOREM 3. <u>There exists extended equilibrium for every economy</u> $E \in \mathscr{E}$, <u>i. e., for all</u> $E \in \mathscr{E}$, $\Phi(E) \neq \phi$.

<u>Proof.</u> First, we check $\mathscr{E}$ is arcwise connected.[7] Let $E, E' \in \mathscr{E}$, we construct $E^t = tE + (1-t)E'$ for $t \in [0, 1]$, i. e., $E^t = (u^t, \bar{x}^t) = (tu + (1-t)u', t\bar{x} + (1-t)\bar{x}')$. By the weak topology given on $\mathscr{E}$, $u^{ht} \in C^1(R_+^\ell \times S, R)$, $\bar{x}^{ht} \in \mathring{R}_+^\ell$ for every agent h. Moreover, u^{ht} satisfies A. 4 for every h and $(u^t, \bar{x}^t)$ satisfies A. 3. Thus, $E^t = (u^t, \bar{x}^t) \in \mathscr{E}$. From Proposition 1 we have the extended equilibrium manifold $\psi_E^{-1}(0) \subset \mathring{R}_+^{\ell n} \times \mathring{S}$ and it is compact. Therefore, the

[7] A topological space X is said to be arcwise-connected if, for each pair of points a, b in X, there exists a path in X with origin a and end point b.

Brouwer degree is defined (for instance, see [13], p. 27). If $E \in \mathscr{R}$, the degree of the map ψ_E is equal to the algebraic sum of the orientations (see [13], p. 26) of the elements of $\psi_E^{-1}(0)$. Let $\deg \psi_E$ denote the degree of map ψ_E. By Proposition 3, there exists $E \in \mathscr{R} \subset \mathscr{E}$, $\deg \psi_E$ is one. Finally, the Brouwer degree is a homotopy invariant,[8] so that $\deg \psi_E$ is one for every $E \in \mathscr{E}$. This implies that $\Phi(E) = \psi_E^{-1}(0) \neq \phi$ for every $E \in \mathscr{E}$. Q E D

COROLLARY 3. *For every convex economy, there is an equilibrium, i.e.,* $W(E) \neq \phi$ *for every* $E \in \mathscr{E}_0$.

Proof. It follows directly from $W(E) = \psi_E^{-1}(0)$ for every $E \in \mathscr{E}_0$. Q. E. D.

[8] Two mappings $f, g: X \to Y$ are homotopic if there exists a continuous map $F: X \times [0, 1] \to Y$ with $F(x, 0) = f(x)$ and $F(x, 1) = g(x)$ for all $x \in X$. To say that Brouwer degree is homotopy invariant is equivalent to saying that any homotopic maps have the same Brouwer degree.

References

1. Abraham, R. and J. Robbin, Transversal Mappings and Flows, W.A. Benjamin, Inc., New York, 1967.

2. Allingham, M.G. and M. Morishima, "Veblen Effects and Portfolio Selection", in M. Morishima, Theory of Demand: Real and Monetary, Oxford, England, 1973, pp. 242-270.

3. Arrow, K.J. and F.H. Hahn, General Competitive Analysis, Holden-Day, San Francisco, 1971.

4. Chichilnisky, G. and P.J. Kalman, "Special Properties of Critical Points and Operators of Parameterized Manifolds in Economics", Journal of Mathematical Analysis and Applications, Feb., 1977.

5. Debreu, G., "Economies with a Finite Set of Equilibria", Econometrica 38, 1970, pp. 387-392.

6. ________, "Smooth Preferences", Econometrica 40, 1972, pp. 603-615.

7. ________, "Regular Differentiable Economies", American Economic Review, May 1976.

8. Dieudonnè, J., Foundation of Modern Analysis, Academic Press, New York, 1960.

9. Hirsch, M.W., Notes on Differential Topology, Department of Mathematics, University of California, Berkeley, 1973.

10. Kalman, P.J., "Theory of Consumer Behavior when Prices Enter the Utility Function", Econometrica 36, 1968, pp. 497-510.

11. Katzner, D.W., "A Note on the Differentiability of Consumer Demand Functions", Econometrica 36, 1968, pp. 415-418.

12. Kelley, J., General Topology, Van Nostrand Co., Princeton, 1960.

13. Milnor, J., Topology from a Differentiable Viewpoint, University of Virginia Press, 1965.

14. Samuelson, P.A., The Foundations of Economic Analysis, Harvard University Press, Cambridge, Mass., 1947.

15. Scitovsky, T., "Some Consequences of the Habit of Judging Quality by Price", Review of Economic Studies 12, 1945, pp. 100-105.

16. Smale, S., "Global Analysis and Economics IIA: Extension of a Theorem of Debreu", J. of Mathematical Economics 1, 1974, pp. 1-14.

17. __________, "Global Analysis and Economics IV: Finiteness and Stability of Equilibria with General Consumption Sets and Production", J. of Mathematical Economics 1, 1974, pp. 119-127.

18. Veblen, T., The Theory of the Leisure Class, Macmillan, New York, 1899.

19. Wallace, A. H., Algebraic Topology: Homology and Cohomology, Benjamin, N. Y., 1970.

OPTIMAL HOUSING SUPPLY OVER TIME UNDER UNCERTAINTY

by

Richard Dusansky and Peter J. Kalman
State University of New York at Stony Brook

I. Introduction

One of the major concerns in urban economics, relevant to both centralized and decentralized economies alike, is the provision of adequate housing in a growing and changing society. Attending singularly to this challenge, this paper presents an analytical model aimed at the achievement of policy-specified housing goals. The model developed emphasizes multiple-goal behavior (i.e., cost cotainment and the achievement of minimum target levels) in a framework of multiple planning options (i.e., demolition, replacement, and rehabilitation of deteriorated structures). Attention is focused on the process of physical deterioration. It is seen that the latter, referred to as "physical filtering," constitutes a stochastic element which seriously complicates planning. Our concern will be with housing supply over time, hence a dynamic framework, and with cost effectiveness, hence the positing of cost minimization. The primary goal of the paper is to demonstrate that it is possible to develop a model which captures the complicated interaction of dynamic and stochastic elements in a multi-choice planning process, and to show that such a model yields operationally implementable solutions.

Section II consists of three parts. In part a, we specify a dynamic objective function which reflects the key cost factors of housing supply. In part b, we develop stochastic constraints which incorporate the housing goals and the physical filtering process. In part c, we construct the formal dynamic and stochastic constrained optimization model. In Section III, we provide a general solution to this model and a useful illustrative example.

II. The General Model

Our starting point is the assumption of the existence of a governmental agency focusing on a community (or region or SMSA) having n initial housing structures. This agency (or general decision making unit) observes, over time, the housing needs of the citizens in the community and the condition of the housing stock. With respect to the latter, it is particularly aware of a dynamic process of decay, and realizes that at various points in time demolition and rebuilding decisions will have to be made. The major goal of the agency is optimal supply of adequate housing over time. We will assume that cost efficiency is a major concern.

We further assume a certain degree of sociological awareness and sensitivity on the part of the agency. Specifically, in terms of our model, this means that consideration will be given to rehabilitation of dilapidated structures, in addition to demolition and replacement. Rehabilitation has the effect of keeping existing neighborhoods intact - in some cities neighborhoods are essentially sub-communities - which may be more desirable than dispersion and regrouping. Rehabilitation is considered as a viable alternative for other reasons as well: rehabilitation may provide better housing for a much larger percentage of the poor, for it is the poor who primarily live in the most deteriorated structures; rehabilitation may more effectively reduce the negative externalities resulting from blighted areas; and rehabilitation may be less costly.

We also assume that the agency defines various housing classifications and chooses minimum class requirements. Then, if specific functional relationships and the associated data are provided, the agency is to decide whether existing structures be rehabilitated or replaced by new structures, and determine the rehabilitation or demolition time schedules in such a way as to best meet the specified housing classification requirements. This is to be done in an optimal way: in a manner consistent with the minimization of costs over time subject to satisfying the specified minimum housing classification requirements.

a. The Dynamic Objective Function

It is important to recognize that each of the current n structures must eventually be acted upon by a decision maker. For example, focusing on the ith initial housing structure ($i=1,\ldots,n$), we observe that it must eventually be demolished and replaced by a new structure, or it must undergo rehabilitation (i.e., the ith initial structure gets replaced in a sense by a rehabilitated structure).[1] In either of these cases the ith initial structure gives way to what is essentially another structure. At some time, however, the fate of this housing structure must also be determined. Once it is, and positive action is taken, we will have yet another structure. We can continue in this way, *ad infinitum,* and describe what is essentially a chain of housing structures which is to be associated with the ith initial housing structure upon which we initially focused. This chain associated with initial structure i we will call the ith housing sequence and denote by H_{ij} the jth housing structure in the ith housing sequence (where $i=1,2,\ldots,n$ and $j=1,2,\ldots,r,\ldots$).

For H_{ij}, we postulate the following operating cost function:

$$\varphi_j^i(u_j^i, \sum_{k=1}^{j-1}\ell_k^i-\ell_0^i+\tau, \tau, c_j^i, m_j^i). \tag{1}$$

u_j^i is the utilization rate of structure H_{ij}. Each apartment unit in the structure has an allowable maximum number of tenants. By summing over the total number of apartment units it is easy to calculate the maximum number of people who can legally inhabit the building. The utilization rate is the ratio of the actual number of tenants to the allowable maximum. The utilization rate, influenced by the number and sizes of families in H_{ij}, has direct implication for maintenance and operating costs.

In the second argument of (1), ℓ_j^i is the age of H_{ij} when it is replaced (where ℓ_0^i is the age of the initial structure in the ith housing sequence at time zero) and τ is the age of H_{ij} $(0 \leq \tau \leq \ell_j^i)$. Thus the expression $\sum_{k=1}^{j-1} \ell_k^i - \ell_0^i + \tau$ is a time variable which serves as a proxy for technology and is a measure of the absolute time t. Specifically, this term specifies, when $\tau = 0$, the time when housing structure H_{ij} first became available for occupancy. That calendar date corresponds to a specific construction technology which has a direct bearing on operating costs. For example, if more efficient systems were available and used, operating costs could be lower than if the technology prevalent decades earlier was dominant. On the other hand, more advanced technology leads to the introduction of entirely new systems - like central air conditioning - the operation of which tends to raise costs. The $\sum_{k=1}^{j-1} \ell_k^i - \ell_0^i + \tau$ variable determines the technological state of the structure.

c_j^i designates the housing classification which structure H_{ij} is in when it becomes available for occupancy ($c_j^i = 1, \ldots, q$ in decreasing order of desirability). Different classifications are often associated with either different operating systems and materials and/or different stages of decay, each of which affect operating costs.

Finally, m_j^i is a parameter which indicates whether structure H_{ij} is new or rehabilitated ($m_j^i = \begin{cases} 1 \text{ if } H_{ij} \text{ is a new structure} \\ 0 \text{ if } H_{ij} \text{ is a rehabilitated structure} \end{cases}$). This may have direct implications for operating costs.

In addition to operating cost, there is one other major category of cost that merits consideration; this is the net investment cost or net capital cost of structure H_{ij}, which has two components. The first component, gross capital costs (denoted by W^i_j), depends on its absolute time of purchase, on its original classification and on whether it was a new or rehabilitated structure. That is,

$$(2)\qquad W^i_j\left(\sum_{k=1}^{j-1}\ell^i_k-\ell^i_0,\ c^i_j,\ m^i_j\right).$$

The second component, salvage value, depends on absolute time of purchase, classification and age at demolition. That is,

$$(3)\qquad S^i_j\left(\sum_{k=1}^{j-1}\ell^i_k-\ell^i_0,\ c^i_j,\ \ell^i_j\right).$$

We are now almost ready to specify the properly discounted cost function associated with the current, incumbent housing structure in the ith housing sequence. But first we must introduce the concept of a "replacement lag." It generally takes time to effect replacement of an existing structure by a new one; it takes time to demolish and to rebuild. This is the replacement lag. The replacement lag associated with H_{ij} will be denoted by γ^i_j.

We now specify the discounted cost function for the ith housing sequence. This is

$$(4)\qquad V^i(u^i_j,\ldots,\ell^i_j,\ldots,c^i_j,\ldots,m^i_j,\ldots)$$

$$= \int_{\ell^i_0}^{\mu^i_1} \varphi^i_1(u^i_1,\tau,\tau,c^i_1,m^i_1)e^{-r\tau}\,d\tau$$

$$- S^i_1(\ell^i_1-\ell^i_0,c^i_1,\ell^i_1)e^{-r(\ell^i_1-\ell^i_0)}$$

$$+ \sum_{k=1}^{\infty} e^{-r[\sum_{j=1}^{k}(\ell^i_j+\gamma^i_j)-\ell^i_0]}\left\{\int_0^{\mu^i_{k+1}} \varphi^i_{k+1}(u^i_{k+1},\sum_{j=1}^{k}\ell^i_j-\ell^i_0+\tau,\right.$$

$$\tau,c^i_{k+1},m^i_{k+1})e^{-r\tau}\,d\tau + W^i_{k+1}\left(\sum_{j=1}^{k}\ell^i_j-\ell^i_0,c^i_{k+1},m^i_{k+1}\right)$$

$$-e^{-r\ell^{i}_{k+1}} S^{i}_{k+1}\Big(\sum_{j=1}^{k+1}\ell^{i}_{j}-\ell^{i}_{0}, c^{i}_{k+1}, \ell^{i}_{k+1}\Big)\Bigg\},$$

$i=1,\ldots,n,$

where $\mu^{i}_{k+1} = \begin{cases} \ell^{i}_{k+1} \text{ if } H_{i\ k+1} \text{ is to be rehabilitated} \\ \ell^{i}_{k+1}+\gamma^{i}_{k+1} \text{ if } H_{i\ k+1} \text{ is to be replaced by a new structure,} \end{cases}$

and where r is the rate of discount.[2] Note that two kinds of discounting are involved in (4). For each housing structure in the sequence we must discount the cost incurred over the structure's lifetime back to its point of initial entry into the sequence. Then we must discount the values associated with all of the entry points back to the present.

Finally, we point out that this expression represents the discounted cost stream associated with the ith housing structure. Recall that we began with n initial structures. Hence to arrive at total current discounted cost, we must sum over the cost streams associated with each of the initial n buildings. That is,

(5) $$V(u^{i}_{j},\ldots,\ell^{i}_{j},\ldots,c^{i}_{j},\ldots,m^{i}_{j},\ldots) = \sum_{i=1}^{n} V^{i}(\cdots).$$

b. Dynamic and Stochastic Constraints: The Process of Filtering and Minimum Housing Requirements

The housing goals of the decision making agency are formalized in the specification of a set of constraints. The agency can establish any finite number of housing (or income) classifications - some examples of these are low-low-income, upper-low-income, lower-middle-income, upper-middle-income, etc., - and specify the minimum number of housing structures to be in each class at any moment of time; these specifications are the housing goals. This general kind of formulation allows for the possibility that the agency may wish to deal with housing supply as it relates to all income classes. Of course, an an obvious special case, the agency can concentrate on low income housing: the minimum requirement for other classes can be set at zero.

Achievement of the specified housing goals over time is seriously complicated by the dynamic process of housing decay, which is the essence of the phenomenon of physical filtering. Housing structures are continuously decaying, and as they decay they move over time from one housing class to another. While each structure undergoes decay, it would be an oversimplification to assume that each decays at the same rate. The rate of decay is clearly influenced by utilization, degree of maintenance and quality of construction, among other factors. Thus the movement from one housing classification to another varies among housing structures. This dynamic and stochastic process complicates the task of the agency. Since the potential for alteration in housing classification exists for each and every structure, the agency must focus careful attention on the changing status of all structures, if the housing objectives are to be satisfied and cost efficiency is to be maintained. The agency must be able to effectively formulate, ideally by relying on a long and diverse history of housing structure decay, probability estimates for various classification changes, and then calculate the relevant expectations.

We will assume, given a sufficiently rich data base, that the agency is able to calculate the appropriate transition probabilities within a reasonable degree of approximation. Specifically, the agency calculates for all structures the relevant $P^{ij}_{k\ell}(\tau)$, the probability of structure H_{ij} going from housing class ℓ to class k when it is of age τ if $c^i_j = \ell$. Having estimated the relevant $P^{ij}_{k\ell}(\tau)$'s, the agency can then calculate the expected number of housing structures in any housing classification k at any time t (denoted by $X_k(t)$, $k=1,\ldots,q$). We can write this as follows:

(6) $$X_k(\ell^i_j,\dots,c^i_j,\dots;t) = \sum_{i=1}^{n}\sum_{z=1}^{\infty}\int_0^{\ell^i_z} P^{iz}_{kc^i_z}(\tau)\,\delta\Big(\sum_{a=1}^{z-1}\ell^i_a-\ell^i_0+\tau-t\Big)\,d\tau,$$

$k=1,\dots,q,$

where $\delta(\cdot)$ is the Dirac delta function defined by the property $\int_A \delta(a)\,da = \begin{cases} 1 & \text{if } a\in A \\ 0 & \text{if } a\notin A \end{cases}$. We first look at the integral. The delta function assures us that, if H_{iz} is not available for tenant occupancy at time t, that is, if t is not an element of the interval $[\sum_{a=1}^{z+1}\ell^i_a-\ell^i_0, \sum_{a=1}^{z}\ell^i_a-\ell^i_0]$, the integral vanishes. However, if t is an element of the interval, that is, if H_{iz} is occupied at time t, the integral becomes

(7) $$P^{iz}_{kc^i_z}\Big(t-\sum_{a=1}^{z-1}\ell^i_a-\ell^i_0\Big)$$

which is the probability that H_{iz} will be in housing class k at time t, when its age is $\tau = (t-\sum_{a=1}^{z-1}\ell^i_a-\ell^i_0)$.

Since at time t, for a given housing sequence i, only one H_{iz} is being occupied, the summation over z will be a stream of zeroes except for one value equal to that in (7), when z is that of the H_{iz} in use at time t.[4] Hence the expression containing the second summation and the integral gives us the expected number of structures in housing class k at any time t in the housing sequence commencing with H_{i1} for any i. Finally by summing over i we arrive at the total expected number of structures in housing class k at time t.

We will assume that the policy maker sets a policy of minimum classification requirements by fixing a set of $\hat{X}_k(t)$, $k=1,\dots,q$, the minimum number of structures in housing class k deemed desirable.[4] For convenience we define

(8) $$\zeta_k(\ell_1^1,\ldots,\ell_j^i,\ldots,\ell_1^n,\ldots,c_j^i;t) = -\hat{X}_k(t)+X_k(\ell_1^1,\ldots,\ell_j^i,\ldots,\ell_1^n,\ldots,c_j^i;t),$$

$k=1,\ldots,q.$

Then the constraint becomes

(9) $$\zeta_k(\cdot;t) \geq 0 \text{ for all } t,$$

$k=1,\ldots,q,$

or equivalently

(10) $$\xi_k(\ell_1^1,\ldots,\ell_j^i,\ldots,\ell_1^n,\ldots,c_j^i) = \min_{0<t<T} \zeta_k(\cdot;t) \geq 0,$$

$k=1,\ldots,q,$

where T is the time horizon of the policy maker, where possibly $T \to \infty$. Thus the original specification of the minimum housing classification constraints is satisfied if expression (10) is satisfied.

c. Formalization of the Model

We now present the formal model. We assume that the decision making agency acts as if to minimize the dynamic cost function in (5) subject to satisfying the dynamic and stochastic housing classification constraints in (10). Specifically we assume that the agency focuses on the problem of

(11) $$\min_{\substack{(\ell_j^i)\\(c_j^i)}} \sum_{i=1}^{n} V^i(\ell_1^i,\ldots,\ell_j^i,\ldots,c_j^i) = \min_{\substack{(\ell_j^i)\\(c_j^i)}} V((\ell_j^i),(c_j^i))$$

subject to

$$\xi_k(\ell_1^1,\ldots,\ell_j^i,\ldots,\ell_1^n,\ldots,c_j^i,\ldots) \geq 0,$$

$$\ell_j^i \geq 0, \; c_j^i \in \{1,\ldots,q\},$$

$$\text{where } V(\cdots) = \sum_{i=1}^{n} V^i(\cdots).$$

Analytic solutions to this model are not easily obtainable for any large n or q except under extreme simplifying assumptions which vitiate the usefulness of the model. A numerical approach would also not be useful because a numerical solution is not feasible, since we have infinitely many decision variables ℓ_j^i and c_j^i. This difficulty can be overcome, however, as we demonstrate in the next section.

III. A General Solution with an Illustrative Example

We will assume that the decision making agency's time horizon is not infinite. This is an eminently reasonable assumption, for it does not preclude the possibility of very long finite horizons. This means that for each i, ℓ_j^i and c_j^i become independent of j for some j sufficiently large. That is,

$$(12) \qquad \ell_j^i = \ell^i, \quad j \geq j_i,$$

and

$$(13) \qquad c_j^i = c^i, \quad j \geq j_i'.$$

The immediate consequence of this step is to reduce the decision variables in (11) to a finite number

$$(14) \qquad N = \sum_{i=1}^{n} j_i + \sum_{i=1}^{n} j_i'.$$

We further assume that the replacement lags are relatively negligible and can thus be deleted from the analysis, and that the m^i variable is of relatively lesser importance in the cost function and can also be deleted. The problem as now stated can easily be solved to any desired degree of accuracy, using standard nonlinear programming techniques, once the functional forms of the φ_j^i's, the S_j^i's, the W_j^i's and the P_{pq}^{ij}'s as well as the values of the u_j^i's, the ℓ_0^i's and r are known.

We will obtain an analytical solution upon specifying some common regularity assumptions. We define a set $A((c_j^i))$:

(15) $$A((c_j^i)) = \{(\ell_j^i) \mid \xi_k((\ell_j^i),(c_j^i)) \geq 0, \ \forall_k, \ \ell_j^i \geq 0 \ \forall_{i,j}\}$$

We make the following assumptions.

<u>Assumption 1</u>: $V^i(\ell_1^i,\ldots,\ell_j^i,\ldots,c_1^i,\ldots,c_j^i,\ldots)$ is an analytical function of all the ℓ_j^i's with continuous first partials.

<u>Assumption 2</u>: For each i and given c_j^i's, the function $\tilde{V}^i(\ell_1^i,\ldots,\ell_{k_i}^i;c_1^i,\ldots,c_j^i,\ldots)$ obtained by setting all ℓ_j^i's with $j>k_i$ equal to $\ell_{k_i}^i$, has one and only one local minimum, no local maximum and no inflection point on the set $\{(\ell_1^i,\ldots,\ell_{k_i}^i)\in R^{k_i} \mid \ell_j^i \geq 0\}$

<u>Assumption 3</u>: The set $A((c_j^i))$ is closed.

<u>Proposition 1.</u> Under assumptions 1 through 3, for a given (c_j^i), the problem of finding an (ℓ_j^i) minimizing $\tilde{V}((\ell_j^i),(c_j^i)) = \sum_{i=1}^{n}\tilde{V}^i(\cdots)$ subject to the constraint $\xi_k((\ell_j^i),(c_j^i)) \geq 0 \ \ \forall_k\in\{1,\ldots,q\}$, has the solution $(\ell_j^i) = (\ell_j^{i*})$, where (ℓ_j^{i*}) is the solution to the unconstrained problem of minimizing $\tilde{V}((\ell_j^i);(c_j^i))$ with respect to (ℓ_j^i), if $(\ell_j^{i*})\in A((c_j^i))$; if not the solution is on the boundary of $A((c_j^i))$.

Proof: Follows directly from assumptions 1, 2 and 3 and the closedness of (15).

We note that assumption 2 will be satisfied for the special case when the functio $\varphi_j^i(\ldots)$, $S_j^i(\ldots)$, $W_j^i(\ldots)$, are certain linear functions. Also from Proposition 1 it follows that if an analytical expression for the boundary of $A((c_j^i))$ can be found, the problem stated therein is reduced to a simple Lagrangian problem. Let the solution be $(\tilde{\ell}_j^i)$, $j=1,\ldots k_i$, $i=1,\ldots,n$, each ℓ_j^i will be a function of (c_j^i). By substituting these functions back into $\tilde{V}((\ell_j^i);(c_j^i))$ we get a function $\hat{V}((c_j^i))$ which now can be minimized over the set of (c_j^i)'s for which $A((c_j^i)) \neq \emptyset$ giving the solution to the original problem (11).

This procedure can be illustrated by an example, an example which will give the reader a feeling for the capabilities of the model. Specifically, we will assume that the cost function is linear in the major variables and that the filtering process can be approximated exponentially.[5] Specifically,

(16) $$\varphi_j^i(\cdots) = \alpha u^i + \gamma\tau + \delta c^i$$

$$W_j^i(\cdots) = \epsilon c^i$$

$$S_j^i(\cdots) = \eta c^i + \iota\ell^i$$

and

(17) $$P^{im}_{kc^i_m}(\cdots) = e^{-k_i\tau}\,\delta_{kc^i} + (1-e^{-k_i\tau})\,\delta_{ki}$$

where $\epsilon > \eta$, $\gamma > -\iota r$, and $\delta_{ij} = \begin{cases} 0 & i\neq j \\ 1 & i=j \end{cases}$.

$V^i(\ell^i,c^i)$ now becomes

(18) $$V^i(\ell^i,c^i) = \left[\frac{\alpha}{r}u^i + \frac{\delta}{r}c^i + \frac{\gamma}{r^2}\right] + \frac{1}{1-e^{r\ell^i}}\left[\left(\frac{\gamma}{r}+\iota\right)\ell^i + (\eta-\epsilon)c^i\right].$$

$\xi_u(\cdots)$ becomes

$$\xi_u((\ell^i),(c^i)) = -\hat{X}_u + \sum_{i=1}^{n} e^{-k_i \ell^i} \delta_{uc^i} \tag{19}$$

Note that $\ell^{i*}(c^i)$ is obtained from (18). From the form of (19), assuming that $k_i = k_i'$, if $c^i = c^{i'}$, we find that

$$A((c_j^i)) = \{(\ell^i) \in R^n \mid \ell^i \geq 0, \ \ell^i \leq \frac{1}{k_i} \ln\left(\frac{\lambda_{c^i}}{\hat{X}_{c^i}}\right)\} \tag{20}$$

where λ_{c^i} is the number of housing structures built into housing class $k = c^i$. Assuming $A((c^i)) \neq \emptyset$ we get $\tilde{\ell}^i(c^i) = \min[\ell^{i*}(c^i), \frac{1}{k_i} \ln(\frac{\lambda_{c^i}}{\hat{X}_{c^i}})]$ Putting this back into $V(\cdots)$ we obtain $\hat{V}((c^i))$ which can easily be minimized over the finite set $\{(c^i) \mid A((c^i)) \neq \emptyset\}$.

IV. Summary

This paper has presented an analytical approach to the problem of providing adequate housing over time. We have constructed a genuinely dynamic model possessing two main features: (1) cost minimization over time as represented by the dynamic objective function and (2) the satisfaction of minimum housing classification requirements over time as represented by the dynamic and stochastic constraints. The latter incorporates in a general way the process of physical filtering which characterizes housing structures, and thus introduces uncertainty formally into the model. A general solution for the constrained optimization model is shown to exist and the capabilities of the model for a realistic case are demonstrated.

Footnotes

1. Of course, the remaining alternative is to do nothing. While a feasible policy decision, it is not within the scope of the problem under study.

2. Of course it is possible to make r dependent on time by writing $r(\sum_{j=1}^{k} \ell_j^i - \ell_0^i + \tau)$. However, this would make our notation even more cumbersome.

3. It is possible for a given moment in time for a chain to be empty, i.e., for no structure in a given housing sequence to be in use. This would be the case if we were in the midst of a replacement lag, where an old structure has been demolished and construction of the new structure which is to take its place is still in process.

4. In this model the dynamic minimum housing targets are exogenous. Ideally, demand forces should be explicitly formulated and the $\hat{X}_k(t)$ be determined by the interaction of supply and demand over time. This formulation, however, lies outside the intended scope of this current paper (which is already considerably complex), but would represent a natural extension of our modeling approach (for the demand structure in this problem is also dynamic and stochastic). We invite others to extend our work in this direction.

5. Linearity assumptions are common in this literature. For example, see [11] and [14]. Also, the assumption of exponential decay over time is also plausible. For example, see [8]. For computational convenience, we assume that $\ell_j^i = \ell^i$, $c_j^i = c^i$, $u_j^i = u^i$, $\ell_0^i = 0$ $\forall j$ and any i. Clearly all of this can be relaxed since there would still be only a finite number of variables.

References

[1] Beckmann, M., "On the Distribution of Urban Rent and Residential Density," Journal of Economic Theory, June 1969.

[2] Beckmann, M., "Applications of a Neoclassical Von Thünen Model to the Housing Market," Annals of Regional Science, June 1962.

[3] Davis, O.A., "A Pure Theory of Urban Renewal," Land Economics, May 1960.

[4] Davis, O.A. and Whinston, A.B., "The Economics of Urban Renewal," Law and Contemporary Problems, Winter 1961.

[5] Dusansky, R. and Kalman, P.J., "Externalities, Welfare and the Feasibility of Corrective Taxes, Journal of Political Economy, September/October, 1972.

[6] Dusansky, R. and Kalman, P.J., "Towards a Dynamic Optimization Framework for Cost-Efficient Urban Renewal," in Urban and Social Economics in Market and Planned Economies, Vol. 2 (ed. by A. Brown, J.A. Licari and E. Neuberger), Praeger, 1974.

[7] Dusansky, R. and Nordell, L., "The Fiscal Implications of An Efficient Public Sector," Annals of Regional Science, June 1972.

[8] Klaassen, L.H., "Some Theoretical Considerations for the Structure of the Housing Market," in Essays in Urban Land Economics, (UCLA: 1966).

[9] Lowry, I.S., "Filtering and Housing Standards: A Conceptual Analysis," Land Economics, November 1960.

[10] Mills, E., Studies in the Structure of the Urban Economy, Baltimore: The Johns Hopkins Press for Resources for the Future, 1972.

[11] Mills, E., "Mathematical Models for Urban Planning," in Urban and Social Economics in Market and Planned Economies, Vol. 1 (ed. by A. Brown, J.A. Licari and E. Neuberger), Praeger, 1974.

[12] Muth, Richard, Cities and Housing, University of Chicago Press, 1969.

[13] Rothenberg, J., Economic Evaluation of Urban Renewal, Brookings Institute: Washington, D. C., 1967.

[14] Rothenberg, J., "Urban Housing Markets: An Analytical Model and Its Applications to the Impact of Rent Control," in Urban and Social Economics in Market and Planned Economics, Vol. 2 (ed. by A. Brown, J.A. Licari and E. Neuberger), Praeger, 1974.

[15] Solow, R. and Vickrey, W.S., "Land Use in a Long Narrow City," Journal of Economic Theory, December, 1971.

List of Symbols

H_{ij}	j^{th} housing structure in the ith housing sequence
u_j^i	the utilization rate of H_{ij}.
c_j^i	housing classification of H_{ij}.
ℓ_j^i	the age of H_{ij} when it is replaced.
τ	the age of H_{ij}, $0 \leq \tau \leq \ell_j^i$.
m_j^i	a parameter indicating whether H_{ij} is new or a rehabilitation; $m_j^i = \begin{cases} 1 \text{ if } H_{ij} \text{ is new} \\ 0 \text{ if } H_{ij} \text{ is a rehabilitation} \end{cases}$
$X_k(\cdot)$	the total expected number of housing structures in any housing class k at any time t.
$p_{km}^{ij}(\tau)$	the probability of housing structure H_{ij} going from housing class m to class k when it is of age τ if $c_j^i = m$.
$W_j^i(\cdot)$	investment cost of H_{ij}.
r	discount rate.
$S_j^i(\cdot)$	salvage value of H_{ij}.
$\varphi_j^i(\cdot)$	operating cost function of H_{ij}.